Simply Delicious

Creative Cooking for the Kosher Kitchen

Mindy Ginsberg

publishing house ת
JERUSALEM ♦]

Cover design: Diane Liff, D. Liff Graphics
Typesetting: Raphaël Freeman, Renana Typesetting

ISBN: 978-965-229-869-0

1 3 5 7 9 8 6 4 2

Gefen Publishing House Ltd.
6 Hatzvi Street
Jerusalem 94386, Israel
972-2-538-0247
orders@gefenpublishing.com

Gefen Books
11 Edison Place
Springfield, NJ 07081
516-593-1234
orders@gefenpublishing.com

www.gefenpublishing.com

Printed in Israel

Send for our free catalog

Library of Congress Cataloging-in-Publication Data

Ginsberg, Mindy.
 Simply delicious : creative cooking for the kosher kitchen / by Mindy Ginsberg.
   pages cm
 Includes index.
 ISBN 978-965-229-869-0
 1. Jewish cooking. 2. Kosher food. I. Title.
 TX724.G5624 2015
 641.5'676--dc23
                      2015022318

Contents

Introduction

Cooking is a creative, fun and rewarding art.

I had no interest in the preparation side of food – only in eating it! – but growing up with the *great taste* of my mother's cooking was the quintessential cooking course. My endeavor to emulate was by trial and error, but with experience and experimentation, cooking became a delightful and gratifying adventure. And the results – well, just ask my family and friends. It doesn't matter how fast the dish disappears from the table as long as it has *the taste.…*

Taste is the key to good cooking.

Recipes are flexible and can be adjusted to your own specific taste. *Elegance is in the presentation.* You can either bring the pot or pan to the table or take that extra step and place the food on a platter or in a bowl with a little garnish. Roast beef is not a prerequisite to elegance. Fish or poultry have endless versatility and boned turkey parts (cut up or chopped) are tastier and healthier.

The daily diet: retain a desired weight by eating in moderation.

- Eat only when hungry.
- Exercise some will power.
- Drink lots of water daily.
- Try to be satisfied with small amounts, like one tablespoon of ice cream, two squares of chocolate or two dried apricots.
- Never take seconds. Put as much as you want to eat on your plate the first time around.
- At affairs, eat half of what's served on your plate. (A friend of mine was told to do this by her dietician. At her next affair she was so busy talking that she ate up the whole plate.

She immediately ordered another portion so that she could leave half over.)

- At the Viennese table, eat only one item, two halves or a taste of three items.
- Weigh yourself only once a week.
- If you're still hungry after the meal, eat a carrot as you leave the kitchen. If you're still hungry have one square of chocolate or the equivalent, and a full glass of water. If you're still hungry then you're losing weight.

I once volunteered for a research study on nutrition. At the interview the entire office staff came with pen and paper to find out how I write cookbooks while still keeping my weight low and steady!

Entertaining

When you're entertaining, decide in advance about the menu, when to shop, which foods can be prepared beforehand and which utensils can be set up beforehand (platters, bowls, serving pieces, coffee cups and cake plates). For eight or more people, seating arrangements will be greatly appreciated.

A few menu pointers:

- **Appetizer & soup**: Soup should be served only after a light appetizer or none at all. If you serve a heavy appetizer and soup, you might as well go straight to dessert.
- **Nibblers**: Carrot and celery sticks, olives, pickles etc.
- **Salad**: For a 3-course meal, keep the salad light (just vegetables).
- **Main course**: Fish or poultry/meat (or a choice of both) together with a few side dishes of carbohydrates and vegetables. *Don't forget color. Think quality rather than quantity.*

- **Dessert**: Occasionally, at dessert time guests remember diets, so make it worthwhile.

Choose quality over quantity. It's like a speech which should be short and to the point. If the audience wants to hear more the speaker will be invited again. So with entertaining: leave something for next time.

A dinner party of 8–10 people is intimate. With a large crowd consider buffet, so that guests don't have to converse only with their neighbors.

Don't be surprised if the guest you planned would be the life of the party had a hard day and keeps falling asleep. For one of my dinner parties I thought I had put together the greatest combination. It turned out the majority were either exhausted, tense or sick. The main topic of conversation was how delicious my food was. That's not such a bad thing but it should be mentioned as a side point.

Don't get upset if a guest eats nothing. Actually he/she can help with the conversation since the mouth is not occupied with chewing.

Don't take it personally if a guest forgot to tell you of a specific diet (vegetarian, macrobiotic, etc.). It's not pleasant, but you did all you could have done. Be sure to have a couple of non-meat dishes available.

Plan beforehand. Don't spend all the time in the kitchen. Prepare every platter, bowl and serving piece, and figure out the logistics of serving before the guests arrive.

Let it all out after the last guest leaves. Don't holler at your co-host (spouse or friend) from across the table if he/she does something that goes against your idea of etiquette. I once attended a home reception for a couple celebrating their fiftieth wedding anniversary. Suddenly, Gertrude screamed *"Louis!"* What Louis did was never revealed, but Gertrude noticed it from the other end of the table.

Don't skimp on ingredients. Remember, taste is the key to a successful meal.

Good luck!

Legumes & More

There's more to legumes than just beans. Legumes, a vegetable protein containing almost all of the essential amino acids, are the edible seeds of leguminous plants – *dry beans, lentils, peas and peanuts*. They're not only high in protein, calcium and dietary fiber, and low in fat and cholesterol, but they're also high in taste and low in cost.

Beans

Beans were one of the first plants cultivated. The farmlands of the kings and noblemen in fifteenth-century England included wheat, barley, oats, rye and beans. The fields were divided into strips, giving each serf a fair share. The herbs, sage, marjoram, rosemary and fennel were found in the kitchen gardens.

Beans are interchangeable except when a specific traditional recipe requires a certain type of bean. The name Boston Bean was derived from Boston Baked Beans; Mexican Chili con Carne calls for red kidney beans, and succotash requires white kidney beans. A three-bean salad should include red kidney beans as one type. Cooked beans can be added to enhance dishes such as pasta, salads, rice, vegetables, meat stews and soups. Cook them and store them in handy packages in the freezer for ready use.

There are many varieties of beans:

- *Adzuke bean* (Phaseolus Angularis): A small, ginger-flavored, oriental bean eaten plain or in a sweetened paste. Though the red variety is the most widely used, it also comes in white, black, gray and mottled varieties.

- *Black bean* (Phaseolus Vulgaris, Turtle Bean): A small, black, oval type of the common bean. A staple food of Cuba, and Central and South America. Creamy texture, tender and sweet tasting. Served with rice, salads, soups and meat stews.

- *Black fermented Chinese bean*: A soybean preserved in salt. Uses: meat and vegetables.

- **Black-eyed bean** (Vigna Cowpea): a small, oval, creamy white Chinese bean with a black or yellow spot. Sold fresh or dried.

- **Barlotto bean** (Phaseolus Vulgaris): Gold with brown flecks. Used in dips and salads.

- **Boston bean family** (Phaseolus Vulgaris): Includes pearl haricot, navy and pea beans. Used in the traditional dish Boston Baked Beans.

- **Canellini bean**: A creamy-white Italian kidney bean. Uses: salads, pasta and soups.

- **Cranberry bean** (Roman Bean): beige with red speckles. Sold fresh or dried.

- **Cocoa bean** (Chocolate): Fermented, roasted and ground from the pod of the tropical cocoa tree. Created by the Mesoamerican civilization and cultivated by pre-Columbian (Maya and Aztec) civilizations.

- **Coffee bean**: First cultivated in Yemen about a thousand years ago. Roasting process: Raw coffee beans are heated to a temperature of approximately 350°–400°F (180°–200°C). The heat causes a loss in water and increase in size. A popping sound occurs, indicating the expansion of gasses inside the bean.

- **Fava bean** (Vicia Faba, Field Bean, Windsor Bean): A small brown bean in the Egyptian variety, and a large brown bean in the American variety. It is known as Broad Bean in Britain. A native of North Africa, it was cultivated by the ancient Greeks and Egyptians. Available fresh, dried or canned. Eaten on its own, or in stews and salads.

- **Flageolet** (Phaseolus Vulgaris): A small green or white kidney shaped bean. Part of the haricot bean family. Native to the Americas. Eaten fresh or dried with meat or rice.

- **Ful Medames** (Lathyrus Sativus): Originated in the Middle East. Very popular in Egypt. Usually baked with eggs, cumin and garlic.

- **Garbanzo Bean** (Chickpeas): A beige bean available whole or split. There are two different types: **Desi**, a small, dark seed, and the more popular **Kabuli**, which has a light color, is larger and has a smoother coat. Uses: stir-fried vegetables, stews and salads. Can be made into humus paste. (See below for cooking instructions.)

- **Great Northern Bean**: A member of the white bean family. Mild flavored, powdery texture. Interchangeable with navy and lima. Uses: soups, casseroles, baked beans, and stews.

- **Haricot Bean**: A term referring to a variety of white beans.

- **Lablab Bean** (Dolichos Lablab, Hyacinth Bean): Indian in origin. Must be shelled before cooking.

- **Lima Bean** (Phaseolus Sativus): Known also as Butter Bean, or Forkhooks when fresh. A native of South America, it is also found in Madagascar. Available fresh, dried or frozen. Served with cooked vegetables, corn (Succotash), soups and casseroles.

- **Marrow Bean**: A member of the white bean family.

- **Mung Bean** (Phaseolus Aureus, Moong Dal, Green Gram): Comes in green, yellow, black or gold and is sold whole, split or skinless. Nutty flavor. Popular for sprouting. Uses: stir-fry vegetables and salads.

- **Navy Bean**: A member of the white bean family. Originally from Italy. Smooth texture, nutty flavor. Uses: baked beans, minestrone soup, and salads.

- **Pigeon Pea** (Cajanus Cajan, Gunga Pea, Toor Dal): A member of the white bean family.

- **Pinto & Pink Bean**: Pink with brown speckles. Can be interchanged with red kidney beans although the kidney beans are larger. Uses: chili, soups, baked beans and stews.
- **Red Kidney Bean**: A sweet bean, ranging from pink to maroon. Uses: salads, rice and meat stews.
- **Rice Bean** (Phaseolus Calcaratus): Native of Southeast Asia. Similar to adzuki bean.
- **Soy Bean**: Round, either cream colored or black. Used whole or processed into flour, bean curd or milk. The yellow variety (Glycine Max) is one of the five sacred beans of ancient China. Cooked in stews, fresh or dried. Can be made into a paste, called Miso.
- **Urd Bean** (Phaseolus Mungo, Urad Dal, Black Gram): A native of India and the Far East. Comes whole or split and skinless.
- **White Kidney Bean**: Comes in various sizes.
- **White Bean Family**: Consists of Great Northern, Cannellini, Navy or Yankee Pea, Pigeon Pea and Marrow Bean.
- **Yankee Bean**: A member of the white bean family.

PREPARING THE BEAN

SOAKING: Soak overnight in enough water to allow room for swelling. Drain and rinse.

TO REMOVE GAS FROM BEANS: Before cooking, place in pot, cover with water, bring to boil, turn off flame and drain. Repeat three times.

TO COOK: Place in pot and add enough water to allow for swelling. Cooking time depends on the specific bean, size and age. Do *not* add salt during cooking time.

NOTE: Dry beans can be stored in a closed glass jar for many months. The older the bean, the drier it becomes, and the more cooking time it will need.

Chickpeas (Garbanzo Beans)

Chickpeas (Garbanzo beans) are in a class of their own.

There are two procedures for preparing chickpeas prior to cooking:

- Soak overnight, covered with a towel, in enough water to allow for swelling. Drain.

- Cook, covered, in lots of water, for 5 minutes. Turn off flame and leave for 1 hour. Drain.

TO COOK: Cook in enough water to allow for swelling (approximately 1 liter [1 quart] water to 1 cup beans) for 1–1½ hours. Time depends on age and desired tenderness. (OPTIONAL: When finished cooking, turn off flame and add 1 teaspoon salt. Stir, and leave until completely cool. Drain.

Suggested seasoning for immediate consumption: salt, pepper, paprika, dried coriander, halved garlic cloves.

Lentils

Lentils, the seeds of a fabaceous plant, come in orange, green, yellow and brown. The Yemenite hilbe is small with a very sharp taste. Puy lentils are dark, French lentils and Indian brown lentils are reddish brown. The orange and Indian brown varieties tend to become puree after cooking.

TO COOK: Scan dry lentils and discard any object not resembling a lentil. Presoak in a bowl with lots of boiled water, covered, for ½ hour. Drain and rinse under cold water.

Lentils can be cooked in two ways:

- Place lentils in pot and add water. The ratio is 1 cup lentils to 4 cups water. Bring to boil, lower flame and cook, covered, for 20 minutes. Turn off flame and let stand for about 10 minutes. Drain.

- For a crunchy consistency, place 1 cup lentils in pot, add 1½ cups boiled water and cook for ½ hour. Let stand for at least 10 minutes.

Cooked lentils can be added in sautéed vegetables, rice, meat stews and pasta dishes. Lentils are delicious by themselves with a nice amount of sautéed garlic and onions, salt, pepper and cumin.

Peas

Peas are generally used in specific recipes.

Types of peas:

- **Blue pea** (Pisum Sativum): Floury texture and retains its shape.

- **Pigeon pea** (Cajanus Cajan, Gunga Pea, Toor Dal): Native to Africa.

- **Split green pea** (Pisum Sativum): Sweeter than the blue pea and becomes puree when cooked. Used in soups and the traditional English pease pudding.

- **Yellow split pea** (Pisum Sativum): Used as a puree for soups and vegetable dishes.

Nuts

There are numerous types of nuts:

- **Peanuts** (Archis Hypogag, Groundnut, Monkey Nut): The only nut that is a legume. Native to South America. The first Spanish explorers in America found peanuts in southeast United States, where it was originally used primarily to feed livestock.

- **Almond** (Rosa Ceae): A member of the peach family. The almond nut is the seed of the almond tree. Originated in Arabia.

- **Brazil nut** (Bertholletia Excelsa): The seed of the Brazil nut tree. Originated and still predominantly grown in the Amazon Valley in Bolivia and Brazil. To shell, roast at 400°F

(200°C) for about 20 minutes. Cool. Crack lengthwise and shell.

- **Cashew nut** (Anacardium): The seed of the cashew tree. Native to coastal areas of Northeast Brazil; introduced to India and Africa by the Portuguese.
- **Chestnut** (Fragaceae) and sweet chestnut (Castenea Sativa): Originated in Southeast Europe and Asia Minor; brought to other areas by the Romans.
- **Chufa nut** (Cyperus Esculenta): Related to the Tigernut; used ground in the Spanish drink Horchata de Chufa.
- **Coconut** (Cocos Nucifera): Fruit of the coconut palm; native to the tropics.
- **Filbert or hazelnut** (Corylus Maxima): Native to the Mediterranean region. To improve flavor, roast at 400°F (200°C) until slightly toasted.
- **Macadamia** (M. Terenifolia, Queensland Nut): Native to Australia.
- **Pine kernel** (Pinus Pinea, Indian Nut): Seed of the stone pine; native to the Mediterranean region.
- **Pistachio nut** (Pistacia Vera): Native to the Middle East and Central Asia.
- **Tigernut (**Cyperus Esculental): Rhizomes (root stem) African plant. Almond flavor.
- **Walnut** (Juglans Regia): Indigenous to Iran.

A nut is a fruit that consists of a seed, which is generally edible, encased in a hard shell. Almonds, pistachios and walnuts were cultivated in Southwest Asia during biblical times. Brazil nuts, cashews and peanuts originate in South America. Early agricultural societies developed techniques of extracting milk, oil and powder from nuts. Oils were extracted from almonds, coconut and walnuts. Nut powder, extracted from almonds and pistachio nuts, originated in Persia and spread east to India and west to the Mediterranean area.

To roast nuts, preheat oven to 200°F (90°C). Spread nuts on baking sheet and roast until delicately brown, stirring occasionally. If desired, sprinkle with salt.

Many recipes call for blanched almonds, meaning almonds with the skin removed. To blanche almonds, boil enough water to immerse all of the almonds. Throw in almonds, turn off flame, and leave for ½ minute. Drain, rinse under cold water, squeeze between fingers and skin should pop off. If skin is completely closed, slit it slightly with a knife. Dry almonds on a baking sheet at 350°F (180°C) for about 5 minutes. To toast, leave in oven for 10 minutes, stirring frequently.

To sauté blanched, halved almonds: Heat oil, add almonds and sauté over medium-low flame a few minutes. Sauté pine nuts with almonds, but add after a couple of minutes, since pine nuts brown faster.

Grains

The varieties of grains are:

- **Barley** (Hordeum Vulgare): Indigenous to the East. Also fermented for malt liquor.

- **Buckwheat groats** (Fagopyrum Esculentum, kasha): Thought to be native of China.

- **Bulgur**: Cracked whole wheat grains. Come in two varieties: coarsely cracked (crunchy texture) and finely cracked.

- **Corn** (Zea Mays, maize, Indian corn): Indigenous to Mexico; *grits* = medium ground corn; *hominy* = coarse ground corn. Used in the processing of bourbon liquor.

- **Millet** (Panicum Miliaceum): Seed of an annual, gluten-free grass.

- **Oats:** (Avena Sativa): Native to Southwest Asia; used in breads and also in the preparation of whiskey (America), gin (Holland) and beer (Russia).

- **Quinoa**: Though technically the botanical fruit of an herb plant (the seed of the chenopadium or goosefoot plant), quinoa is treated as a grain. Originating in the South American Andes, the Incas called it the "mother grain." Ranges in color from off-white to off-black. The lighter color is considered superior. High in protein, calcium, iron, vitamin E and various Bs.

- **Sago**: From the sago and palm trees in the Far East. Used as an invalid food in milk, puddings, and in Scandinavian dishes such as the Danish Sagosuppe (sago soup).

- **Semolina**: Particles from hard durum wheat. Used in puddings. When mixed with water, forms into minute pellets knows as couscous.

- **Whole wheat grains**: Comes in two sizes. The smaller size is called "green whole wheat grains," and takes a little less time to cook. To cook regular-size grains: place 1 cup grains in pot, add 2 cups water, and cook, covered, for 1 hour. Leave for ten minutes. Drain, if necessary.

Rice

Varieties of rice (Orzya Sativa) are:

- **Basmati**: Grown in the foothills of the Himalayas. Soak before cooking.

- **Glutinous (glue-like)**: Gluten free. Widely used in Chinese cooking and in processing beer. Becomes sweet and sticky.

- **Brown**: Parboiled to remove surface starch, thus leaving most of the vitamins and nutrients in the grains.

- **Italian**, brown & white: Large, round grain; used in the Italian dish, Risotto.

The Subtle Flavor of Herbs, Spices & Seeds

Subtle flavor is the ultimate in elegant, gourmet cooking. Salt and pepper give the taste; herbs, spices and seeds bring out that distinctive flavor. Amounts and types used depend on individual taste. Don't overdo it. The idea is to feel the taste, not eat it.

Herbs are derived from leaves of annual and perennial shrubs, of which there is a large variety:

- **Basil**: Flavor is enhanced when cooked. Pots of fresh basil leaves may keep flies away. Used in eggplant, fish, soup, tomato dishes, vinaigrette dressing, zucchini

- **Bay leaves**: Derived from the laurel tree (a symbol of glory for poets and heroes, hence the term "Poet Laureate"). Used in artichokes (placed in cooking water), bouquet garni (see below), pickling stews, tomato sauce, tomato soup, vegetable soup. Discard when done.

- **Bouquet garni**: A mixture of dried marjoram, parsley, bay leaves and rosemary. Used in stews and soups. Wrap in cheese cloth and discard when done.

- **Chervil**: Parsley family. Improves flavor of other herbs when used together. Used in fish, poultry, salads, soups, vegetables.

- **Chives**: Mild onion. Used in poultry, salads, sauces, soups, stews, potatoes, stuffing.

- **Coriander** (cilantro, Chinese parsley [Coriandrum sativum]): Herbaceous plant. Used in cheddar cheese, cream cheese, pickling, pot roast, pasta, rice dishes, guacamole, soups, stews.

- **Dandelion**: Roots are used as a coffee substitute. Used in fresh salad, spinach.

- **Dill** (Anethum graveolens): Opiaceous plant. Used in pickling, cheese dips, pasta, salads, potatoes, soups.

- **Garlic** (Allium sativum): Liliaceous plant. Used in practically all non-sweet dishes.
- **Marjoram** (sweet): Mint family (usually used together with thyme). Used in bouquet garni, meat, omelet, potatoes, salads, sauces, soups, stews, stuffing, vegetables.
- **Oregano**: Wild marjoram. Used in barbecue marinades, bouquet garni, eggplant, fish, poultry, spinach, soups, stews, stuffing, tomato dishes, pizza.
- **Parsley** (Petroselinum crispum): Used in fish, meat, salads, soups.
- **Rosemary** (Rosmarinus officinalis): Menthaceous shrub. Traditional symbol of remembrance. Use sparingly. Used in barbeque marinades, bouquet garni, fish, poultry, spinach, stuffing.
- **Sage** (Salvia officinalis): Menthaceous shrub. Use sparingly.
- **Tarragon** (Artemisia Dracunculus): Also known as estragon. Used in eggs, fish, mushrooms, poultry, salads, sauces, spinach, tomato dishes.
- **Thyme** (a menthaceous plant): Usually used together with marjoram. Used in cheese dishes, fish, meats, onions, potatoes, sauces, soups, stews, stuffing.
- **Turmeric** (Curcuma longa): Aromatic rhizome of an East Indian zingiberaceous plant, lily family. Causes yellow coloring. Used in curries, rice, pickling, vegetables.

Spices

Spices are derived from the bark, fruit and berries of perennial plants. Spices include:

- **Allspice** (Pimenta officinalis): Myrtaceous tree, berry of the pimiento tree. The scent resembles a combination of cloves, cinnamon and nutmeg. Used in pickling, sweet and sour fish.

- **Cayenne pepper**: Ground sharp red pepper. Use sparingly. Used in cheeses, sauces, barbecue sauces, meat, soups, stews.
- **Cinnamon**: Inner bark of any of several lauraceous trees of the genus cinnamonum. Used in coffee and yeast cakes, desserts, meat, sweet rolls.
- **Cloves**: Dried buds. Use sparingly. Used in broths, meat, pickling, sweet and sour fish, sweet rolls.
- **Cumin** (Cuminum cyminum): Small apiaceous plant, carrot family. Used in barbeque sauces, soups, lentil dishes, cheeses, chili, chopped meat, eggs, pickling.
- **Curry**: Mixture of herbs and spices, usually including turmeric and coriander. Used in oriental dishes, rice.
- **Ginger**: Rhizome of any of the reed-like plants of the genus zingiber. Native to East Indies. Used in certain cakes, cookies, fish, oriental dishes, puddings, soups, vegetables.
- **Mace**: Outer nutmeg covering. Used in certain cakes, cookies, fish, meat, stews.
- **Nutmeg** (Myristica fragrans): Seed of the fruit of an East Indian tree. Used in garnish to sweet milk drinks, desserts, puddings, quiche toppings, soups.
- **Paprika**: Hungarian pepper. Used in dressings, onions, poultry, sauces, soups, stews.
- **Pepper**: White, green and black variations. The darker the variation, the stronger the flavor. Most dishes that call for salt can use a little pepper, except cakes.
- **Saffron**: Stigma of a crocus plant (also called vegetable gold). Use sparingly.

Seeds

- **Caraway**: Used in breads, cabbage, cheese, chopped meat, sauces, potato salad.

- **Cardamom**: Ginger family. Pungent taste. Black, green and white variations. The lighter the color, the better the taste.

- **Fennel** (Foeniculum vulgare): Umbelliferous plant. Relative to dill. Mild licorice taste. Used in cabbage dishes, fish, lentils, pickling, poultry, meat, salads, stir-fried vegetables.

- **Mustard, seeds**: Used in pickling.

- **Mustard, prepared**: Used in dressings, fish, meat, poultry, mayonnaise.

- **Poppy**: Used in breads, certain cakes, cookies, pastries.

- **Sesame** (Sesamum indicum): Herbaceous plant. Used in breads, breading mixture (e.g., breaded chicken, fish), garnish for vegetable dishes.

Other Seasonings

- **Capers**: Green hyssop buds. Used in fish, salads, sauces for fish, tartar sauce dressing.

- **Cream of tartar**: Derived from grape juice after fermentation. Reacts with baking soda to produce carbon dioxide, which assists in the rising process of dough and in beating egg whites.

- **Salt**: Used in cakes (a pinch of salt enhances taste, reduces acidity and increases the sweetness of sugar), cooked fruit (a pinch of salt added to the cooking water brings out the maximum sweetness of the fruit), most dishes (salt gives the taste).

Salads

Avocado-Cashew Salad

2 avocados	¼ cup lemon juice
1 tsp prepared mustard	1 tsp salt
1 Tbsp honey	⅛–¼ tsp black pepper
⅓ cup olive oil	2 Tbsp cashew nuts, cut up

Cut up avocados into bowl. Add rest of ingredients and toss. Garnish with orange wedges.

Avocado-Pecan Salad

1 avocado	½ red pepper
2 hard-boiled eggs	3 pickles
2 medium tomatoes	1 Tbsp lemon juice
1 small sweet onion	2 Tbsp pecan nuts, broken up
2 scallions	Vinaigrette Dressing (page 36)
1 Tbsp chopped parsley	

Cut up avocado, eggs and vegetables as desired, and place in large bowl with lemon juice and pecan nuts.

Pour desired amount of Vinaigrette Dressing over salad and toss.

Beet Salad with Pecans

1½ lb. (750 g) beets

1 onion, sliced

½ cup chopped parsley

DRESSING

2 Tbsp each olive oil and red wine vinegar

1 Tbsp lemon juice

1½ tsp salt

¼ tsp black pepper

1 Tbsp cumin powder

2 Tbsp pecan nuts, broken up

Wash beets well. Cut into quarters and cook in lots of water until tender (about 40 minutes). Drain.

Leave for about 15 minutes until it's possible to work with them.

Peel and slice beets.

Place them in a large bowl and add onion slices and parsley.

DRESSING: In small bowl mix ingredients together. Pour over beets and toss.

Refrigerate at least a few hours before serving.

Broccoli-Nut Salad

2 lb. (1 kg) broccoli, raw, parboiled or cooked (as desired)

3 scallions, cut up

½ cup broken-up pecan nuts

½ cup peanuts, halved

3 tangerines sectioned (remove hard membranes from outside)

DRESSING

½ cup apple or wine vinegar

½ cup sugar

¾ tsp salt

½ tsp dried coriander

½ cup mayonnaise

Cut up broccoli and place in bowl with scallions, nuts and tangerine sections.

DRESSING: Mix ingredients together. Add to broccoli and toss.

VARIATION: Use Vinaigrette Dressing (page 36) instead.

Bulgur-Walnut Salad

Preferable to prepare a few hours or a day before.

1 cup bulgur	**DRESSING**
1½–2 cups boiling water	⅓ cup lemon juice
2 scallions, cut up	¼–⅓ cup olive oil
1 cup chopped parsley	1 tsp salt
⅓ cup chopped mint leaves	¼ tsp black pepper
⅓ cup walnuts, cut up	½ tsp turmeric

There are two methods of preparing coarsely cracked bulgur:

- Place 2 cups bulgur in bowl, add 3 cups water, cover, and leave for 1 hour. Drain if necessary.
- Cook 2 cups bulgur with 4 cups water for 7 minutes. Turn off flame and leave for 10 minutes.

To prepare finely cracked bulgur, place 2 cups in bowl, add 3 cups water, cover, and leave for ½ hour.

Combine bulgur, scallions, parsley, mint and walnuts in bowl.

DRESSING: Shake ingredients in jar and place in bowl. Pour over bulgur and toss.

Bulgur with Sunflower Seeds & Almonds

1 cup bulgur

1½–2 cups boiling water

¼ cup each chopped parsley and dill

2 Tbsp sunflower seeds

2 Tbsp almonds, blanched and slivered

DRESSING

2 Tbsp sunflower seed oil or olive oil

2 Tbsp lemon juice

½ tsp salt

⅛ tsp black pepper

1 tsp sugar

½ tsp each dried tarragon and coriander

Two methods of preparing coarsely cracked bulgur:

- Place 1 cup bulgur in bowl, add 1½ cups water, cover, and leave for 1 hour. Drain if necessary.
- Cook 1 cup bulgur with 2 cups water for 7 minutes. Turn off flame and leave for 10 minutes.

To prepare finely cracked bulgur, place 1 cup in bowl, add 1½ cups water, cover, and leave for ½ hour.

Add parsley, dill, sunflower seeds and almonds to bulgur.

DRESSING: In jar, shake all ingredients. Pour over bulgur salad and toss.

Cabbage Salad with Sesame Seeds & Almonds

1 Tbsp sesame oil

¼ cup almonds, blanched and slivered

2 Tbsp pine nuts

1 small cabbage, coarsely grated

3 carrots, grated

½ cup bean sprouts

2 cucumbers, peeled and grated

½ red pepper, diced

2 Tbsp sesame seeds

DRESSING

2 Tbsp soy sauce

¼ cup vinegar

2 Tbsp sesame oil

¼ cup sugar

1 tsp salt

Heat sesame oil over medium-low flame. Add almonds and sauté a few minutes, stirring continuously, until golden. Add pine nuts and sauté another couple of minutes until golden, stirring continuously. (Nuts will darken when left in oil.)

In large bowl combine cabbage, carrots, bean sprouts, cucumbers, red pepper, sesame seeds and sautéed almonds and pine nuts.

DRESSING: Shake ingredients in jar, pour over vegetables and toss.

Refrigerate a few hours.

Cabbage-Noodle Salad

1 medium cabbage, grated

8 oz. (200 g) noodles, cooked

4 scallions, cut up

½ cup each of sesame seeds, sunflower seeds and slivered almonds

DRESSING

2 Tbsp soy sauce

¼ cup sugar

¼ cup red wine vinegar

Place cabbage, noodles, scallions, seeds and almonds in bowl.

Mix dressing ingredients. Pour over salad and toss. Refrigerate a few hours.

Chicken Salad with Fruit & Nuts

1 whole chicken breast, marinated and grilled

Romaine lettuce, cut up

2 ripe mangoes, diced

2 ripe pears, diced

½ cup dried cranberries

½ cup broken-up walnuts

2 Tbsp broken-up cashew nuts

½ cup cooked chickpeas (optional)

Vinaigrette Dressing (page 36)

To marinate and grill chicken breast, see "Marinades for Poultry" (page 109).

Place salad ingredients in large bowl. Add enough Vinaigrette Dressing to give it the quintessential taste. Toss.

Couscous Salad with Walnuts

1 cup + 2 Tbsp water

2 Tbsp olive oil

1 tsp salt

1 cup quick-cooking couscous

4 cloves garlic, crushed

A few cherry tomatoes, halved

½ red pepper, diced

1 few black olives, pitted and cut up

¼ cup each chopped parsley and dill

1 Tbsp red wine vinegar

½–1 tsp dried basil

⅛ tsp black pepper

2 Tbsp ground walnuts

Place water, olive oil and salt in medium-size pot. Bring to boil over medium flame.

Add couscous, mix and let stand for 10 minutes.

Fluff up with fork to separate grains.

Add rest of ingredients and mix well.

Serve warm or at room temperature.

VARIATION: Prepare couscous as directed. Add sautéed pine nuts, raisins and dill and toss.

Fennel-Orange Salad

2 medium oranges, cut up

1 small red onion, sliced

1 large fennel, sliced

A couple of leaves of Romaine lettuce, cut up

2 Tbsp pecans, broken

DRESSING

1 Tbsp wine vinegar

⅓ cup olive oil

½ tsp salt

⅛ tsp black pepper

2 cloves garlic, crushed

Place oranges, red onion, fennel, lettuce and pecans in a large bowl.

DRESSING: Shake all of the ingredients in a jar, pour over vegetables and toss.

Rice & Garbanzo Bean Salad

1 cup cooked garbanzo beans (chickpeas)

1½ cups cooked rice (= ½ cup uncooked rice)

⅓ cup each red, green and yellow peppers, diced

¼ cup cut-up scallions

¼ cup Roquefort cheese

2 Tbsp pecan nuts

DRESSING

1 tsp each of salt and sugar

⅛ tsp black pepper

½–1 tsp cumin powder

¼ tsp each dried tarragon and turmeric

2 Tbsp sesame seeds

3 Tbsp olive oil

2 tsp lemon juice

Place garbanzo beans, cooked rice, peppers and scallions in bowl.

DRESSING: In small bowl combine salt, sugar, pepper, cumin powder, tarragon and turmeric. Pour into jar. Add rest of dressing ingredients and shake well.

Pour dressing over salad. Add Roquefort cheese and toss.

Place in serving bowl and sprinkle with pecan nuts.

Quinoa-Nut Salad I

1 cup water

½ cup quinoa

1 cup corn kernels

2 scallions, cut up

2 carrots, grated

1 red pepper, diced

2 Tbsp chopped mint leaves

½ cup each of chopped parsley and chopped dill

½–1 cup dried cranberries

1 clementine, cut up

1 small avocado, cut up (optional)

2 Tbsp each of sunflower and sesame seeds

¼–½ cup pecans, cut up

¼ cup lemon juice

Vinaigrette Dressing (page 36)

Run quinoa through strainer under water for about 15 seconds to remove bitterness.

Bring 1 cup water to boil. Add quinoa and cook, over low flame, for 12 to 13 minutes. Let sit for 10 minutes.

Place quinoa in bowl, add remaining ingredients with enough dressing to give it taste and mix.

Quinoa-Nut Salad II

2 cups water	Grated lemon rind
1 cup quinoa	3 Tbsp honey
1 cup cooked corn kernels	3 Tbsp pine nuts
¼ cup chopped mint leaves	¼–½ cup cashew nuts, cut up
1 scallion, cut up	1 tsp salt
¼ cup lemon juice	Vinaigrette Dressing (page 36)

Run quinoa through strainer under water for about 15 seconds to remove bitterness.

Bring 2 cups water to boil. Add quinoa and cook, over low flame, for 12 to 13 minutes. Let sit for 10 minutes.

Place quinoa in bowl, add remaining ingredients with enough dressing to give it taste and mix.

Quinoa-Nut Salad III

2 cups water	½ cup each of dill and parsley, cut up
1 cup quinoa	
2 scallions, cut up	¼ cup craisins (dried cranberries)
1 Granny Smith apple, diced	½ cup cashew nuts, cut up
1 onion, diced	Vinaigrette Dressing (page 36)

Run quinoa through strainer under water for about 15 seconds to remove bitterness.

Bring 2 cups water to boil. Add quinoa and cook, over low flame, for 12 to 13 minutes. Let sit for 10 minutes.

Place quinoa in bowl, add remaining ingredients with enough dressing to give it taste and mix.

Lentil-Walnut Salad

1 cup lentils	3 Tbsp balsamic vinegar
1½ cups boiled water	2 Tbsp olive oil
½ cup walnuts, cut up	1 tsp salt
4 scallions, cut up	¼ tsp black pepper
½ cup parsley	

Cook lentils in water for ½ hour. Drain, and place in bowl.

Preheat oven to 350°F (180°C). Roast walnuts for about 3 minutes.

Add to lentils with rest of ingredients and mix.

Spinach-Nut Salad

1 lb. (½ kg) fresh spinach, washed and dried

½ lb. (250 g) snow peas

2 mandarin oranges, cut up

1 cup Chinese noodles

¼ cup each pine nuts and cut-up cashews

DRESSING

¼ cup olive oil

½ cup cider or wine vinegar

⅓ cup brown sugar

½ tsp salt

Cut the spinach into strips. Place the salad ingredients in bowl.

In small bowl combine dressing ingredients. Pour over salad and toss.

Tahini (*Tehina*) Spread

3–4 cloves garlic	1 tsp salt
½ cup parsley	¼ tsp black pepper
1 cup pure tahini (*tehina*) paste	1 tsp ground zatar (optional)
1 cup water	½ tsp ground ginger
½ cup lemon juice	

Mince garlic in food processor.

Add rest of ingredients and process until smooth.

3-Bean Salad with Pecans

1 cup each kidney and black-eyed beans	5 cloves garlic, minced
2 cups green beans, cut up and cooked	¼ cup pecan nuts, broken up
2 sweet onions, thinly sliced	About ¾ cup Vinaigrette Dressing (page 36)

Soak beans overnight in enough water to allow for expansion. Drain and rinse.

Place beans in pot, add enough water to allow for swelling and cook for about 2 hours.

Drain. Place in large bowl, add rest of ingredients and toss.

Vegetable, Bean & Pasta Salad

Preferable to prepare a day in advance.

3–4 Tbsp olive oil

5 cloves garlic, minced

2 onions, sliced

½ each red pepper and green pepper, cut into strips

2 fennel bulbs, thinly sliced

1 tsp paprika

2 tsp salt

¼–½ tsp black pepper

1 tsp each dried coriander, basil and tarragon

½ lb. (250 g) pasta, cooked

2 carrots, grated

½ cup corn kernels

1 cup cooked beans

½ cup cooked garbanzo beans (chickpeas)

1 tomato, diced

¼ cup dried cranberries

1 tomato, diced

½ cup each chopped parsley and chopped dill

1 Tbsp lemon juice

¼ cup almonds or pecans, broken up

¼ cup pine nuts

Vinaigrette Dressing (page 36)

In large frying pan or wok heat oil and stir-fry garlic, onions, red and green pepper, fennel and paprika for about 7 minutes, stirring continuously.

In small bowl mix together salt, pepper, coriander, basil and tarragon.

Place pasta in large bowl. Add rest of ingredients.

Add enough Vinaigrette Dressing to give a good taste and mix well.

Note: Ingredients are flexible. Add or subtract according to your taste.

VARIATION: Add 1½ cups flaked cooked salmon and 1 avocado, diced.

Whole Wheat Grain Salad with Nuts

Preferable to prepare a day before.

2 cups whole wheat grains

4 cups water

1 red onion, diced

¾ cup sun-dried tomatoes, softened and cut up

2 cucumbers, diced

¼ cup cooked soy beans (optional)

¾ cup dried cherries or cranberries

½ cup chopped parsley

¼ cup each cashew nuts and peanuts, broken up

¼ cup each sunflower and sesame seeds

DRESSING

⅓–½ cup lemon juice

1 Tbsp prepared mustard

2 Tbsp olive oil

1 Tbsp honey

2 tsp salt

½ tsp black pepper

½ tsp dried tarragon

Cook whole wheat grains in water for 1 hour. Drain, if necessary. (The grains will have a crunchy texture).

Place in large bowl with red onion, tomatoes, cucumbers, soy beans, cherries/cranberries and parsley. (To soften sun-dried tomatoes, soak in hot water for about 20 minutes and pat dry.)

DRESSING: Shake in jar and pour over salad. Toss.

At serving time mix in cashews and peanuts.

Whole Wheat Grain Salad with Almonds

1 cup whole wheat grains

2 cups water

½ cup chopped dill

1 scallion, sliced

¼ cup almonds, coarsely chopped

DRESSING

¼ cup olive oil

2 Tbsp wine vinegar

1 tsp salt

¼ tsp black pepper

½ tsp dried coriander

2 Tbsp sesame seeds

Cook whole wheat grains in water for 1 hour. Leave for 10 minutes. Drain, if necessary. (The grains will have a crunchy texture).

In large bowl mix together whole wheat grains, dill, scallion and almonds.

DRESSING: Shake all the ingredients in a jar. Pour over salad and toss.

Whole Wheat Grains & Pecans

1 cup whole wheat grains

2 cups water

2 Tbsp olive oil

1 large onion, thinly sliced

6 cloves garlic, minced

1 red pepper, cut into strips

½ cup string beans, julienne

¼ cup pecans, cut up

SEASONING

1 tsp salt

¼ tsp pepper

½ tsp each dried basil, thyme and marjoram

Cook whole wheat in water, covered, for 1 hour.

Turn off flame and leave for 15 minutes. Drain, if necessary.

Meanwhile, stir-fry vegetables and nuts in heated olive oil.

In small bowl mix together all of the seasoning.

Add vegetables and seasoning to whole wheat and toss.

Vinaigrette Dressing

4 cloves garlic, minced

¼ cup red wine vinegar

2 Tbsp water

⅔ cup olive oil

2 tsp salt

½ tsp black pepper

1 tsp paprika

2 Tbsp prepared mustard

1 Tbsp Worcestershire Sauce (optional)

2 tsp dried basil

2–3 tsp sugar

In food processor, mince garlic first and then add rest of ingredients.

Soups

Lentil Soup with Nuts

2 cups green lentils

2 Tbsp olive oil

4 cloves garlic, crushed

2 onions, chopped

2 tsp paprika

8 cups water

2 carrots, grated

1 nob celery, grated

¼ cup chopped dill

1 tomato, chopped

1 Tbsp each of lemon juice, brown sugar, wine vinegar

½ cup dry red wine

2½ tsp salt

½ tsp each black pepper, dried basil, ginger, thyme and marjoram

Ground almonds

Pine nuts

Sift through lentils and remove anything that doesn't resemble a lentil.

Place lentils in a bowl. Add enough boiled water to allow for swelling. Cover, and leave for ½ hour. Drain and rinse. In large, flat-bottomed pot heat olive oil and sauté garlic and onion for about 10 minutes, adding paprika a few minutes into the sautéing.

Pour lentils into pot together with water, carrots and celery. Cook for 45 minutes.

Add dill, tomato, lemon juice, brown sugar, wine vinegar and wine, and cook for another 30 minutes.

Meanwhile, in small bowl mix together salt, pepper, basil, ginger, thyme and marjoram. When soup is done, stir in seasoning.

Leave soup to cool somewhat.

Puree soup in blender a little at a time, or with portable blender stick.

Sprinkle individual portions with almonds and pine nuts.

Split Pea Soup with Pine Nuts

2 cups split peas

½ cup pearl barley

10 cups water

1 Tbsp paprika

2 Tbsp oil

6 cloves garlic, crushed

2 onions, diced

2 stalks celery, diced

3 carrots, chopped

4 tsp salt

¼ tsp black pepper

½ tsp ginger

2 tomatoes (1 cup), crushed

½ cup dry red wine

2 Tbsp oil

Pine nuts and croutons

3 frankfurters (meat or vegetarian), sliced (optional)

Cook split peas, barley, water and paprika for 1½ hours.

Meanwhile, sauté garlic and onions in oil for about 10 minutes. Add to soup after the 1½ hours, together with the celery and carrots. Continue cooking for another hour.

Turn off flame. Add salt, pepper, ginger, tomatoes and wine and stir. (Tomatoes can be crushed in food processor.)

Sauté pine nuts in heated oil over medium-low flame for a few minutes.

Sprinkle individual portions with pine nuts, croutons and frankfurters.

Soup will thicken when left standing. Add a little boiled water until you get the desired consistency.

Pumpkin Soup with Nuts

About 1 lb. (500 g) pumpkin, diced

2 yams, diced

1 carrot, diced

2–3 Tbsp oil

2 onions, diced

5 cloves garlic, crushed

1 tsp paprika

¼ cup cut-up fresh dill

5½ cups water

2 tsp salt

½ tsp each black pepper, thyme and marjoram

½ tsp ginger

1 tsp cumin powder (optional)

½ cup dry red wine

GARNISH

Walnuts and pecans, coarsely chopped

Croutons

(Pumpkin, yams and carrots should add up to 6–7 cups.)

In large flat-bottomed pot, sauté onion and garlic in heated oil for about 10 minutes. Add paprika a few minutes into the sautéing.

Add pumpkin, yams, carrots, dill and water. Bring to boil and cook for ½ hour. Turn off flame.

Meanwhile, in small bowl, combine seasoning ingredients together.

When soup is done, add seasoning and wine and stir until blended.

Let soup cool somewhat.

Blend with portable blender (or in regular blender 2 cups at a time).

Heat and serve.

Sprinkle individual portions with a little extra dill and walnuts, pecans and croutons.

Legumes & Pasta

Bean Stew

Vegetarians can leave out the meat entirely. If so, adjust seasoning to desired taste and add flour at end of sautéing time for a little thickness.

1 lb. (½ kg) lean beef, dark turkey meat or chicken breasts

2 Tbsp flour

2 Tbsp oil

SEASONING

1 tsp salt

¼ tsp pepper

½ tsp each of dried oregano, ginger and coriander

2 tsp cumin powder

6 cloves garlic, minced

1 onion, diced + 2 onions, cut into wedges

1 cup mushroom caps

1 red pepper, cut into strips

1 carrot, cut into strips

1 cup cooked beans (your choice)

1 Tbsp prepared mustard

1 tsp paprika

½ cup dry red wine

2 scallions, cut up

2 tomatoes, cut into wedges

1 cup tomato juice

¼ cup pine nuts

Preheat oven to 350°F (180°C).

Cut meat into strips and pat dry. Sprinkle flour over meat and mix.

In wok or frying pan, heat oil and brown meat over medium-high flame, turning occasionally until all sides are brown.

In small bowl mix seasoning together. Set aside.

Add garlic and diced onion, and fry another few minutes. Add onion wedges, mushrooms, red pepper, carrot, beans, mustard, and paprika and sauté for about 10 minutes, stirring occasionally.

Add wine and continue sautéing another few minutes. Mix in scallions, tomatoes, tomato juice, pine nuts and seasoning.

Transfer to a deep casserole dish and bake in oven.

BAKING TIME: Lean beef will need 45 minutes. Turkey meat will need 30 minutes. Chicken breasts may not need any baking time.

NOTE: Sautéing and baking for stir-fried vegetables is a matter of taste. Some like crunchy half-cooked vegetables, while others prefer them soft and fully-cooked.

Garbanzo Beans with Rice & Almonds

½ cup garbanzo beans
(chickpeas)

2 Tbsp olive oil

⅓ cup almonds, blanched and
halved

¼ cup pine nuts

SEASONING

1 tsp salt

¼ tsp pepper

½ tsp dried coriander

2 tsp curry powder

1 cup rice, cooked

Soak garbanzo beans overnight, covered with towel, in enough
water to allow for swelling, Drain.

Cook the beans, covered, in enough water to allow for
expansion, for 1–1½ hours. (Time depends on age of bean and
desired tenderness.) Drain.

Sauté almonds in heated olive oil over low-medium flame for a
few minutes, stirring occasionally.

Add pine nuts and sauté for at least minute or two. Turn off
flame when light brown. (Beware of burning; they will darken
while cooling.)

In small bowl, combine seasoning ingredients.

In large bowl, mix together garbanzo beans, nuts, rice, and
seasoning.

Fava Beans with Garlic & Pecans

½ lb. (250 g) fava beans

water

2 Tbsp olive oil

3 cloves garlic, minced

½ tsp salt

⅛ tsp pepper

½ tsp turmeric

GARNISH

2 Tbsp pecan nuts, cut up

Soak beans overnight in enough water to allow for swelling. Drain.

Place beans in pot (large enough to allow for swelling). Cover with lots of water. Cook, covered, for about 1½ hours, until soft. (Cooking time depends on age and size of beans.) Drain.

In large bowl, mix together olive oil, garlic, salt, pepper and turmeric.

Add beans and mix. Refrigerate.

TO SERVE: Sprinkle with pecan nuts.

VARIATION: A mixture of red kidney and haricot beans can be substituted for fava beans.

Succotash with Pine Nuts

1 cup cooked garbanzo beans (chickpeas)

2 cups cooked white lima beans

3 cups cooked corn kernels

¼ cup (2 oz., 50 g) butter

1 red pepper, slivered

3 carrots, sliced and cooked

1 tsp salt

¼ tsp chili powder

1 cup sweet cream

2 Tbsp pine nuts

Place beans and corn in large bowl.

In saucepan, melt butter and sauté red pepper.

Pour over beans and corn. Add rest of ingredients and mix.

P.S. I use corn kernels from fresh cooked corn. For easier removal of kernels, cook corn a few days before, freeze, and thaw out. Kernels will fall off individually.

TIME SAVER: Cook beans whenever you have the time. Divide them into about 100 g packages and freeze them for ready use.

Vegetable-Bean Slow-Cooking Stew

3 Tbsp oil

2 onions, sliced

6 cloves garlic, minced

1 Tbsp paprika

SEASONING

2½ tsp salt

¼–½ tsp pepper

2 tsp cumin powder

2 tsp turmeric

½ tsp ginger

¾ cup garbanzo beans (chickpeas)

¾ cup white beans

¼ cup barley

¾ cup whole wheat grains

2 carrots, sliced

2 potatoes, quartered

2 yams, cut into chunks

Boiling water

In large pot heat oil and sauté onions and garlic for about 10 minutes, stirring occasionally.

Add paprika a few minutes into the sautéing.

In small bowl, combine seasoning ingredients.

Add seasoning and rest of ingredients. Pour boiling water to more than cover the stew. Bring to boil, lower flame and cook for 2 hours. Add dumplings (see next recipe) for last hour of cooking.

Place in oven at 225°F (110°C), and bake overnight (approximately 10 hours).

Dumplings

2 Tbsp oil	1 egg
2 onions	½ tsp salt
1½ cups flour	⅛ tsp pepper
⅓ cup bread crumbs	

Sauté onions in heated oil.

Mix together all of the ingredients in a bowl.

Add a little water if too thick.

Form into oblong balls.

Put in pot for the last hour of cooking time (before placing stew in oven).

Lentils with Pecans

1 cup green lentils

1½ cups boiled water

2 Tbsp oil

5 cloves garlic, minced

1 large onion, diced

2 tsp paprika

½ cup red pepper, slivered

1 lb. (½ kg) zucchini, sliced

½ lb. (250 g) mushrooms

1½ tsp salt

¼ tsp pepper

½ tsp each of dried thyme, marjoram, tarragon, ginger and coriander

1 Tbsp cumin powder

¼ cup pecan nuts, broken up

In bowl, soak lentils in a pot with enough boiled water to allow for swelling, covered, for ½ hour. Drain. Return to pot and add 1½ cups boiled water. Cook, covered, for 20 minutes. Let stand for 10 minutes.

In heated oil, over medium-high flame, sauté garlic, onion and paprika for 10 minutes, stirring occasionally. Add red pepper, zucchini and mushrooms and continue sautéing for another 10 minutes. Add lentils and toss.

In small bowl, mix all of the seasonings. Sprinkle over vegetables together with pecan nuts and toss.

P.S. If you don't have all of the herbs, don't worry. They all add flavor, but the lentils will be tasty even with just salt, pepper and cumin.

Lentil-Pecan Pate

1 cup green lentils	½ tsp paprika
1½ cups boiled water	3 hardboiled eggs
¼ cup olive oil	1–1½ tsp salt
3 cloves garlic, minced	¼ tsp pepper
4 onions, chopped	1 cup pecan nuts, ground

In bowl, soak lentils in pot with enough boiled water to allow for swelling, covered, for ½ hour. Drain. Return to pot, add 1½ cups boiled water and cook for 20 minutes. Leave for 10 minutes.

Heat olive oil in skillet and sauté garlic and onions for about 10 minutes, stirring occasionally. Add paprika a few minutes into the sautéing.

In food processor, with metal blade, process lentils, onion mixture, eggs, salt and pepper.

Place in bowl, add pecan nuts and mix until smooth.

Soy Bean–Cashew Spread

2 cups cooked soy beans
(reserve ⅓ cup liquid)

2 cloves garlic, minced

⅓ cup soy bean liquid

2 Tbsp olive oil

½ tsp salt

¼ tsp ginger

¼ tsp chili powder (optional)

2 Tbsp cashew nuts

Process all the ingredients in food processor until smooth.

MAKING IT EASIER: Cook 2 cups raw soy beans, divide them into 2 cups + ⅓ cup broth portions and freeze for future use.

P.S. Cooked soy beans can also be added to all kinds of dishes, such as stir-fried vegetables, rice, pasta dishes and salads.

Lentils with Rice & Nuts

1½ cups green lentils

2½ cups boiled water

1 cup rice

3 Tbsp olive oil

3 onions, sliced

8 cloves garlic, minced

2 tsp paprika

Salt and pepper

1 Tbsp cumin powder

¼ cup dry white wine

2 Tbsp pine nuts

¼ cup almonds, blanched and halved

1 tsp curry

In pot, soak lentils with enough boiled water to allow for swelling, covered, for ½ hour. Drain. Return to pot, add 2½ cups boiled water and cook for 20–30 minutes. Leave for 15 minutes.

Cook rice. Set aside.

Sauté onions and garlic in heated olive oil for 10–15 minutes. Add paprika a few minutes into sautéing. Add ½ tsp salt and ¼ tsp pepper and mix.

Add cumin, wine, pine nuts and ¾ of the sautéed onion to lentils and mix until well blended.

Sauté almonds in a little heated olive oil over medium-low flame for a few minutes, until golden. (Beware of burning; almonds will darken when left in oil.) Add almost all the almonds to rice together with 1 tsp salt, ¼ tsp pepper and curry.

On serving platter form a ring of rice and pile up lentils in center. Arrange remaining sautéed onions around lentils. Sprinkle extra almonds over lentils.

VARIATION: add ⅓ cup cooked adzuke or kidney beans to rice.

Humus Spread with Pine Nuts

1 cup garbanzo beans (chickpeas)	1 tsp each salt and cumin powder
¼ cup olive oil	¼ tsp pepper
⅔ cup cooking liquid	¼ cup tahini spread
	2 Tbsp pine nuts

Soak beans overnight in enough water to allow for expansion, covered with towel. Drain.

Cook beans in a lot of water for 1–1½ hours. Drain, reserving ⅔ cup liquid.

Allow beans to cool slightly. Process in food processor with metal blade.

Add olive oil, cooking liquid and seasoning and process until smooth.

Place in bowl, add tahini spread and pine nuts and mix.

TO SERVE: Garnish with sliced tomatoes, onion, pickles and olives.

Lentils, Pasta & Pine Nuts

½ cup green lentils

2 Tbsp olive oil

5 cloves garlic, minced

1 onion, chopped

2 carrots, grated

1 cup of any vegetable stock or water

SEASONING

1 tsp paprika

½ tsp each curry powder, dried rosemary, thyme, basil, ginger and marjoram

2 tsp salt

¼–½ tsp pepper

3 tomatoes, chopped

½ cup dry or semidry white wine

¼ cup pine nuts

½ lb. (250 g) pasta

½ cup cooked adzuke beans

Soak lentils in enough boiled water to allow for swelling, covered, for ½ hour. Drain.

In frying pan sauté garlic, onion and carrots in heated olive oil for 5 minutes. Add stock and lentils. Bring to boil and cook, covered, over low heat for 15 minutes.

In small bowl, combine seasoning ingredients. Add seasoning, tomatoes and wine and continue cooking for another 10 minutes. Add pine nuts and stir.

Cook pasta, drain, rinse, and drain a little more. Mix into lentils together with beans.

Pasta, Broccoli & Pecans

1 lb. (500 g) broccoli	2½ tsp salt
3 Tbsp olive oil	¼–½ tsp black pepper
3 cloves garlic, minced	2 tsp dried coriander
1 large onion, diced	¼ tsp sugar
3 tomatoes, pureed	¼ cup each of pine nuts and
¼ cup dry white wine	broken pecan nuts
	½ lb. (250 g) pasta

In pot, cover broccoli with water. Add 2 tsp salt, bring to boil and cook, covered, over low-medium flame for 5 minutes. Remove with slotted spoon and drain. (Leave stock in pot to cook pasta with.) Cut broccoli into small pieces.

In saucepan sauté garlic and onion in heated oil for 10 minutes.

Add broccoli, tomatoes, wine, salt, pepper, coriander and sugar and simmer for 10 minutes.

Add pine nuts and pecans and mix.

Meanwhile, boil the stock (if more liquid in needed, add water) and cook pasta.

Drain and rinse. Mix into broccoli mixture.

Noodle-Vegetable Mix with Pecans

2–3 Tbsp oil

1 lb. (500 g) grated cabbage

2 onions, sliced

6 cloves garlic, minced

½ each red and green pepper

2 carrots, grated

½ lb. (250 g) medium noodles

Handful each chopped dill and parsley

SEASONING AND SEEDS

1½–2 tsp salt

¼–½ tsp black pepper

½ tsp each ginger and turmeric

1 Tbsp each caraway and sesame seeds

2 Tbsp white wine

2 Tbsp pecan nuts, cut up

Sauté cabbage, onion, garlic, red and green peppers, and carrots.

Cook noodles as directed and place in bowl. Add cabbage together with dill and parsley.

In small bowl combine seasoning ingredients and seeds.

Add to noodles together with wine and pecans. Mix well.

Spaghetti with Garlic & Pine Nuts

1 lb. (500 g) spaghetti

3 Tbsp olive oil

8 cloves garlic, minced

3 Tbsp pine nuts

¼ cup each chopped dill, parsley and basil leaves

2 tsp salt

¼–½ tsp black pepper

1½ tsp dried coriander (optional)

In large pot cook spaghetti as directed until al dente. Drain and rinse well.

In same pot sauté garlic and pine nuts in olive oil a few minutes. (Do not preheat oil.) Stir almost continuously to prevent sticking and burning.

Return spaghetti to pot. Add the garlic and pine nuts, dill, parsley and basil.

In small bowl mix together salt, pepper and coriander. Add to spaghetti and toss until well blended.

Noodle Kugel with Pecans

½ cup chopped pecan nuts

¼ cup brown sugar

2 Tbsp margarine, room temperature

8 oz. (200 g) medium noodles, cooked

3 eggs

½ cup sugar

½ tsp salt

½ tsp cinnamon

Preheat oven to 350°F (180°C).

In small bowl combine pecans, brown sugar and margarine.

Place around bottom of greased Bundt pan.

Combine noodles, eggs, sugar, salt and cinnamon, and pour over pecan mixture.

Bake for about 1 hour.

When cool, loosen all sides with flat knife and turn over onto platter.

Vegetables

Asparagus with Mayonnaise-Mustard Dressing

12 asparagus

MAYONNAISE-MUSTARD DRESSING

½ cup mayonnaise

3 Tbsp mustard

2 Tbsp ground almonds

If asparagus are not precut, break the bottom of each one with your hands.

TO COOK ASPARAGUS: Place asparagus in boiling water (enough to cover asparagus), with a bit of salt. Cook for about 3 minutes. Pour off water and plunge asparagus into iced water. Drain.

Broil for 2–3 minutes on each side. Beware of burning.

Remove carefully with slotted metal spatula and place on platter.

Serve at room temperature with dressing.

Broccoli-Potato Pie with Pine Nuts

⅓ recipe Plain Pastry I (page 131)

MUSHROOM MIXTURE

3 Tbsp oil	½ lb. (250 g) mushrooms, sliced
2 onions, diced	1 tsp salt
4 cloves garlic, crushed	¼ tsp black pepper
1 Tbsp paprika	

BROCCOLI MIXTURE

1 lb. (½ kg) broccoli, cooked and chopped	2 Tbsp each sesame seeds, pine nuts and wheat germ
¼ onion, diced	
2 cloves garlic, crushed	½ tsp salt
1 egg, beaten	⅛ tsp pepper
2 Tbsp chopped dill	
2 lb. (1 kg) potatoes, peeled, cooked and mashed	

Preheat oven to 350°F (180°C).

Roll out and place pastry dough in 10" (25 cm) deep pie dish. Set aside.

MUSHROOM MIXTURE: In heated oil, over medium-high flame, sauté onions, garlic and paprika for 10 minutes. Add mushrooms and continue sautéing for another 10 minutes over medium flame. Mix in salt and pepper. Set aside.

BROCCOLI MIXTURE: Combine ingredients for broccoli mixture. Spread over pie shell.

Mix ½ of the onion-mushroom mixture together with dill into mashed potatoes and spread over broccoli. Sprinkle rest of onion-mushroom mixture on top.

Bake for 30 minutes.

Cabbage & Nuts

1 cabbage, coarsely grated

2 Tbsp oil

3 cloves garlic, crushed

2 onions, diced

2 tsp paprika

SEASONING

1–1½ tsp salt

¼ tsp black pepper

½ tsp each turmeric, dried oregano and caraway seeds

2 tsp lemon juice

1 tsp sugar

2 tomatoes, pureed

1 cup cooked haricot beans (optional)

2 Tbsp pecans, coarsely chopped

1 Tbsp peanuts, halved

Soften cabbage by microwaving it for about 6 minutes.

In heated oil, sauté garlic, onions and paprika for 10 minutes, stirring occasionally.

Add cabbage and sauté another 10 minutes.

In small bowl, combine seasoning ingredients.

Add seasoning and rest of ingredients and toss.

MAKING IT EASIER: In your spare time cook a bunch of beans, divide them into small portions and freeze for ready use.

Cabbage & Walnuts

1 cabbage, coarsely grated

¼ cup (50 g) butter or olive oil

3 cloves garlic, crushed

1 onion, chopped

1 Tbsp chopped dill

1 tsp salt

⅛ tsp black pepper

1 tsp dried coriander

½ cup vermouth or dry white wine

1 cup walnuts, coarsely chopped

In frying pan sauté cabbage, garlic and onion in heated butter or oil for about 5 minutes.

Add dill, spices and vermouth and continue sautéing for another 5 minutes.

Add walnuts and sauté for about 2 minutes more.

Red Cabbage with Pecans & Cashews

2 Tbsp oil

3 cloves garlic, crushed

1 onion, diced

1 red cabbage, coarsely grated

1 cooking apple, grated

¼ cup strawberry jam

2 Tbsp brown sugar

½ cup lemon juice

1 tsp salt

¼ tsp black pepper

¼ cup pecans, cut up

2 Tbsp cashew nuts

In large pot sauté garlic and onion in heated oil for about 10 minutes.

Add rest of ingredients (except nuts) and cook, covered, for 40 minutes.

Mix in nuts.

Red Cabbage with Marmalade & Nuts

2 Tbsp oil

1 large onion, diced

1 red cabbage, coarsely grated

2 Tbsp brown sugar

⅓ cup cider vinegar

⅓ cup water

2 tsp salt

½ tsp orange marmalade

2 Tbsp pecans, cut up

2 Tbsp peanuts, halved

Heat oil in large pot and sauté onion for about 10 minutes.

Add rest of ingredients (except nuts), cover and cook for 45 minutes, stirring occasionally.

Mix in pecans and peanuts.

Corn Fritters

1½ lb. (750 g; about 4 cups) cooked corn kernels

¾ cup flour

2 tsp baking powder

½ tsp salt

⅛ tsp chili powder (optional)

½ cup sugar

3 eggs, beaten

1–2 Tbsp butter, melted

Butter or oil, for frying

Maple syrup (optional)

If using fresh corn, cook corn on the cob. Allow to cool; then remove corn kernels with sharp knife. Be sure to separate kernels that stick together.

(MAKING IT EASIER: Corn may be cooked beforehand and frozen. When thawed out the corn kernels will fall off individually.)

In large bowl, sift together flour, baking powder and salt. Add corn, chili powder, sugar, eggs and melted butter and mix.

Heat butter or oil in pan. Over medium flame drop corn batter by tablespoonfuls and fry on both sides. Add butter or oil to pan as necessary.

Drain corn fritters on paper toweling.

Serve with maple syrup.

Cauliflower & Pecans

SEASONING:

½ tsp salt	3 Tbsp olive oil
⅛ tsp black pepper	1 red pepper, slivered
½ tsp each turmeric and coriander	1 medium cauliflower, cut up
	¾ cup water
1½ tsp cumin powder	2 Tbsp cut up parsley
¼ tsp cayenne pepper (optional)	½ cup pecans, broken

In a small bowl, combine seasoning ingredients.

In wide pot, heat oil. Add red pepper and seasoning and sauté for about 2 minutes, stirring occasionally. Add cauliflower florets and stir until vegetables are well coated.

Add water and cook, covered, for 30 minutes.

Add parsley and pecans and mix. Let settle for about 10 minutes.

Cauliflower with Curry & Nuts

1 head cauliflower florets, cooked

2 Tbsp shelled sunflower seeds

¼ cup walnuts, broken

2 Tbsp peanuts, halved

DRESSING

3 cloves garlic, crushed

1 small onion, diced

¼ cup olive oil

¼ cup wine vinegar

¼ cup each chopped parsley and dill

½ tsp prepared mustard

¼ tsp salt

⅛ tsp black pepper

½ tsp curry powder

Place cauliflower florets, seeds and nuts in large bowl.

Process dressing ingredients in food processor with metal blade or shake vigorously in jar. Pour over cauliflower mixture and toss.

Refrigerate for a few hours.

Celery with Olives & Nuts

4 stalks celery

⅓ cup pitted olives

1 onion, sliced

1 tsp paprika

½ tsp salt

1 tsp each turmeric and cumin powder

1 Tbsp sesame seeds

½ cup walnuts, cut up

Remove strings from celery by breaking in half and discarding loose strings.

Cut up celery.

[TO PREPARE OLIVES: Place in small pot, cover with water, bring to a boil and drain.]

Place celery, olives and onion in pot, cover with water and cook, covered, for 1 hour.

Drain and return to pot.

In small bowl mix together paprika, salt, turmeric, cumin powder and sesame seeds. Add to pot together with walnuts, and stir over low heat for a few minutes to dry out.

Green Beans with Curry & Almonds

1 lb. (½ kg) green beans, cut into small pieces

1 Tbsp oil

4 cloves garlic, crushed

½ tsp salt

¼ tsp black pepper

1 tsp curry powder

3 Tbsp sesame seeds

2 tsp lemon juice

1 tsp sugar

¼ cup almonds, blanched and slivered

Cook green beans until almost soft. Drain and pat dry on paper toweling.

In large frying pan or wok heat oil. Add green beans with rest of ingredients (except almonds) and sauté a few minutes. Stir in almonds.

Serve warm or at room temperature as a salad.

Mushrooms with Cumin & Pecans

3 Tbsp olive oil

3 cloves garlic, crushed

1 onion, diced

SEASONING

½ tsp each salt, dried thyme and paprika

¼ tsp black pepper

1 tsp cumin powder

⅛ tsp cayenne pepper (optional)

1 lb. (500 g) mushroom caps, quartered

2 Tbsp chopped parsley

2 Tbsp pecans, cut up

In frying pan sauté garlic and onion in heated oil for about 10 minutes.

In small bowl mix together all of the seasoning.

Add mushroom and seasoning to onions and continue sautéing for about 10 minutes.

Add parsley and pecans and stir together.

Stuffed Mushrooms with Pistachio Nuts

½ lb. (250 g) mushrooms

STUFFING

2 scallions, diced

4 cloves garlic, crushed

2 Tbsp chopped parsley

½ tsp each salt, dried tarragon, thyme and marjoram

⅛ tsp black pepper

1 Tbsp sesame seeds

2 Tbsp pistachio nuts, crushed

2 Tbsp grated cheese

Remove mushroom stems and set mushroom caps aside. Chop stems.

STUFFING: Sauté chopped mushroom stems with scallions, garlic, and parsley for about 5 minutes.

In small bowl mix together salt, tarragon, thyme, marjoram and pepper. Add seasoning mixture, sesame seeds, pistachio nuts and grated cheese to sautéed vegetables and mix.

Fill mushroom caps with stuffing.

Microwave for about 5 minutes.

Onions & Nuts

¼ cup (50 g) butter

3 large onions, sliced

½ tsp salt

⅛–¼ tsp black pepper

¼ tsp dried tarragon

1 Tbsp caraway seeds

2 Tbsp pine nuts

2 Tbsp walnuts, coarsely chopped

Preheat oven to 350°F (180°C).

Melt butter in pot, over low flame. Add onions, salt, pepper, tarragon, caraway seeds and pine nuts and stir.

Spread onto shallow baking pan and bake for about 1¼ hours.

Add walnuts and mix.

Potato Roll with Mushrooms

4 medium potatoes, peeled and cooked

2 Tbsp butter

5 cloves garlic, minced

2–3 onions, diced

½ lb. (250 g) mushrooms, diced (optional)

2 tsp salt

¼–½ tsp black pepper

1 tsp caraway seeds (optional)

2 Tbsp chopped dill

1 recipe Plain Pastry I (page 131)

Preheat oven to 350°F (180°C).

Mash potatoes.

In large frying pan, heat butter over low flame.

Increase heat and sauté garlic and onions for about 10 minutes, stirring occasionally.

Add mushrooms and sauté for another 10 minutes, stirring occasionally.

In a small bowl, mix salt, pepper and caraway seeds.

Add to potatoes along with mushroom mixture and dill. Mix together.

Divide pastry dough into 3 pieces and roll out.

Fill each piece of dough with about ⅓ of potato filling. Be sure not to overstuff. Fold in sides and roll up carefully.

Place on greased cookie sheet and bake for about 50 minutes.

Serve all by itself or together with creamed spinach.

Pumpkin & Peanuts

1 Tbsp oil

1 lb. (½ kg) pumpkin, thinly sliced

½ tsp salt

½ tsp cinnamon

1 Tbsp lemon juice

½ tsp sugar

¼ cup walnuts, cut up

2 Tbsp peanuts, halved

Sauté pumpkin in heated oil for a few minutes.

Add salt and cinnamon and continue sautéing until pumpkin is soft, stirring occasionally.

Add lemon juice, sugar and nuts and continue sautéing for another minute.

Pumpkin Cake with Apples & Nuts

1¼ cups flour

1 tsp baking powder

1 tsp baking soda

¼ tsp salt

½ tsp cinnamon

½ cup oil

½ cup brown sugar

1 egg

1½ tsp vanilla extract

¼ tsp almond extract

1 Tbsp water

1 Tbsp lemon juice

2 cooking apples, grated

1 lb. (500 g) pumpkin, finely grated

1 carrot, finely grated

¼ cup walnuts, coarsely chopped

CRUMB TOPPING

2 Tbsp butter

1 Tbsp brown sugar

¼ cup ground walnuts

½ cup oatmeal

½ tsp cinnamon

Preheat oven to 350°F (180°C).

In bowl sift flour, baking powder, baking soda, salt and cinnamon. Set aside.

In mixer, at medium speed, beat oil and brown sugar.

Add egg and extracts and beat until thick.

Reduce speed to lowest and add flour mixture alternately with water and lemon juice. The batter will be thick.

Squeeze out water from apples. Add apples, pumpkin and carrot to mixer a little at a time, or fold in with wooden spoon. Fold in walnuts.

In small bowl mix together crumb-topping ingredients.

Pour batter into flat, greased baking dish.

Sprinkle crumb topping over cake and bake for about 45 minutes.

Creamed Spinach with Sesame Seeds & Pine Nuts

2 lb. (1 kg) spinach, cooked and chopped

SAUCE

⅓ cup flour, sifted

1½ tsp salt

¼ tsp pepper

⅛ tsp dried coriander

⅛ tsp cayenne pepper (optional)

¼ cup (50 g) butter

1 cup heavy sweet cream

1½ cups milk

2 Tbsp dry red wine

2 Tbsp sesame seeds

¼ cup pine nuts

Place spinach in large bowl.

SAUCE: In bowl mix flour, salt, pepper, coriander and cayenne pepper.

In saucepan, over low flame, melt butter. Remove from flame and stir in flour mixture.

Return to stove. Over medium-low flame slowly add cream, milk and wine, and cook, stirring continuously, until the sauce thickens.

Turn off flame and allow to settle for about 15 minutes.

Add sauce to spinach together with sesame seeds and pine nuts. Mix.

Roasted Potatoes with Walnuts

16 (3 lb.; 1½ kg) baby potatoes

¼ cup oil

8 cloves garlic, crushed

2 large onions, sliced

2 tsp paprika

2 tsp salt

¼ tsp pepper

½ tsp ginger

2 Tbsp walnuts, cut up

¼ cup each chopped parsley and dill

½ cup smoked meat (optional)

Preheat oven to 425°F (220°C).

If using larger potatoes, cut into quarters.

In frying pan or wok, sauté garlic and onions in heated oil for about 10 minutes. Add paprika a few minutes into the sautéing.

In small bowl mix together salt, pepper and ginger.

Add potatoes and seasoning mixture to onions and mix until well coated.

Place in flat baking pan so that potatoes are on one level.

Cover and bake for 20 minutes. Uncover and stir gently.

Lower oven to 350°F (180°C) and bake for about another hour. Stir gently once during the roasting time.

Remove from oven.

Sprinkle with walnuts, parsley, dill and smoked meat and mix.

Roasted Potatoes with Pecans

1½ lb. (750 g) baby or small potatoes

1 lb. (500 g) onions (small, large or both)

SAUCE

2 Tbsp oil

1 Tbsp soy sauce

2 Tbsp honey or brown sugar

2 Tbsp prepared mustard

2 Tbsp ketchup

¼ cup chopped dill

5 cloves garlic, crushed

¼ tsp pepper

1 tsp zatar (optional)

¼ cup roasted pecan nuts, cut up

If using small potatoes, cut into quarters.

Onions may be small or large. Small onions can be whole or halved; large onions should be quartered or cut into wedges.

In large bowl, mix sauce ingredients together.

Fold potatoes and onions into sauce until well coated.

FOR TERRA-COTTA BAKING PAN: Do not preheat oven. Rinse baking pan under cold water before adding food. Grease bottom of pan and add vegetables. Cover. Bake at 350°F (180°C) for 20 minutes.

Increase heat to 425°F (220°C) and bake for 1 hour.

When removing from oven place on cushioned, straw or wooden trivet (*not* metal).

 FOR REGULAR PAN: Preheat oven to 425°F (220°C). Follow directions for Roasted Potatoes with Walnuts (see previous recipe).

Mix in pecans just before serving.

TO ROAST PECAN NUTS: Preheat oven to 350°F (180°C). Place on flat pan and roast for 10 minutes.

Potato Pancakes (Latkes)

6 potatoes	2 tsp salt
1 small onion, finely grated	¼–½ tsp black pepper
3 eggs	Oil, for frying

Grate potatoes very fine. Plunge into ice water. Drain.

Place in large bowl and add rest of ingredients. Mix well.

Heat frying pan with lots of oil. Drop by large spoonfuls and fry, on both sides, until brown.

Drain on paper toweling.

Serve with sour cream or applesauce.

Note: Latkes can be frozen. Place on cookie sheet side by side. Layer, with waxed paper between each layer. To reheat, preheat oven to 400°F (200°C). Place each layer of wax paper on a separate cookie sheet. Cookie sheets may be put in the oven straight from the freezer. Place cookie sheets in oven side by side and reheat for 10–15 minutes, until latkes are sizzling.

Potato-Rice Pie

SEASONING

1 Tbsp salt

½ tsp black pepper

1 tsp curry

2 cups basmati rice

2 cups boiled water

½ cup cooked adzuke beans

¼ cup chopped dill

3–4 Tbsp olive oil

1 potato, thinly sliced

½ tsp turmeric

¼–½ cup boiled water

In small bowl mix together salt, black pepper and curry. Set aside.

Pour rice into 2 cups boiled water and cook for 10 minutes.

Drain in strainer and mix in beans, dill and seasoning.

Spread olive oil in a 3–4 quart (3–4 liter) Teflon pot. Grease sides.

Spread potato slices in pot, and sprinkle with turmeric.

· Add rice and ¼–½ cup boiled water.

Cover with cotton dish towel, and then with pot cover.

Cook for 25 minutes on medium-low flame. Raise heat for last 5 minutes.

Allow to settle for 10 minutes.

Turn over onto large round platter.

Quinoa with Stir-Fried Veggies & Cashews

1 cup quinoa

2 cups boiled water

2 Tbsp oil

1 large onion, diced

½ each green and red pepper, cut into strips

1 large carrot, grated

4 cloves garlic, minced

2 scallions, cut up

¼ cup chopped parsley

2 Tbsp sesame seeds

SEASONING

1½ tsp salt

¼ tsp black pepper

½ tsp ginger

1 tsp turmeric

½ cup cooked chickpeas (optional)

½ cup broken-up cashews

Rinse quinoa in strainer for about 15 seconds. Allow to drain for a few minutes.

In heated pot, dry out quinoa for a few minutes, stirring continuously, until a slight popping sound is heard. Lower flame, slowly add boiled water, and cook for 12–13 minutes. Let stand for 10 minutes.

Meanwhile, in heated oil, stir-fry onion, peppers and carrot. Once soft, add garlic, scallions, parsley and sesame seeds and fry for a few more minutes.

In small bowl mix seasoning ingredients.

Add vegetables, seasoning, chickpeas and cashews to quinoa and mix.

Spinach-Potato Roll with Pine Nuts

1 recipe Plain Pastry I (page 131)

FILLING

2 Tbsp butter or oil

4 cloves garlic, minced

1 onion, chopped

2 tsp paprika

½ lb. (250 g) spinach, cooked and chopped

1½ lb. (750 g) potatoes, peeled, cooked and mashed

1½ tsp salt

¼ tsp black pepper

½ tsp each dried coriander and ginger

3 Tbsp each chopped parsley and dill

2 Tbsp pine nuts

1 Tbsp caraway seeds

2 Tbsp cream or milk

⅓ cup grated Cheddar cheese

Preheat oven to 350°F (180°C).

Divide pastry dough into 3 pieces. Set aside.

FILLING: In heated butter or oil sauté garlic, onion and paprika for 10 minutes, stirring occasionally. Combine with rest of filling ingredients.

Roll out each piece of dough, spread with ⅓ of filling, fold in sides and roll up.

Place on greased cookie sheet and bake for 50 minutes.

Yams with Pecans

3 lb. (1½ kg) yams, cubed and cooked

2 Tbsp sugar

¼ cup honey

½ cup milk

1 egg

3 Tbsp butter, melted

1 tsp vanilla extract

TOPPING

½ cup brown sugar

½ cup flour

3 Tbsp butter

½ cup pecans, cut up

Preheat oven to 350°F (180°C).

Mash yams and add sugar, honey, milk, egg, butter and vanilla.

Spread into flat pan.

Mix topping ingredients together and sprinkle over yams.

Bake for about 25 minutes.

Yams with Dried Apricots & Walnuts

2 lb. (1 kg) yams	⅓ cup apricot liquid
¾ cup dried apricots	¾ cup brown sugar
¼ cup butter	¼ cup walnuts, cut up
1 tsp grated orange rind	

Preheat oven to 375°F (190°C).

Parboil yams, remove skin and slice.

Cut apricots into quarters and soak in boiled water for 15 minutes.

Melt butter in saucepan. Once melted, add orange rind and apricot liquid and stir a few seconds over low flame, until smooth.

Arrange yams in deep 2½ quart (2 liter) casserole dish. Sprinkle brown sugar over yams, and then pour sauce on.

Cover and bake for 40 minutes.

Top with nuts for last 5 minutes.

Yams with Pineapple

2 lb. (1 kg) yams

⅓ cup pecans, cut up

1¼ cups canned crushed pineapple

2 Tbsp butter

¼ cup juice from can of pineapple

2 Tbsp brown sugar

¼ tsp salt

TOPPING

2 Tbsp butter, softened

⅓ cup oatmeal

1 Tbsp brown sugar

Scrub yams, place in pot, cover with water, and cook until soft. Remove with slotted spoon. Peel and cut into medium slices.

Preheat oven to 425°F (220°C).

Spread yams onto flat, large, greased baking pan. Sprinkle with pecans and pineapple, making sure to reserve the pineapple juice.

Melt butter in saucepan. Add pineapple juice and heat. Pour over yams.

Sprinkle with brown sugar and salt.

Mix topping ingredients together in bowl. Sprinkle over yams.

Bake for 15 minutes.

Fish

Baked Halibut with Cheddar & Almonds

2 lb. (1 kg) halibut, trimmed and skinned

½ cup lemon juice

¼ cup vermouth, or dry or semidry white wine

¼ cup butter or olive oil

½ cup grated cheddar cheese

½ cup bread crumbs

4 cloves garlic, crushed

½ tsp each salt, dried thyme and marjoram

¼ tsp black pepper

TOPPING

½ cup butter or olive oil

½ cup almonds, blanched and halved

Coat halibut with lemon juice and leave in pan for an hour.

Rinse and pat dry. Pour out lemon juice and rinse pan.

Preheat oven to 425°F (220°C).

Pour vermouth or wine onto bottom of pan and place halibut on top.

Melt butter in medium saucepan. Remove from flame. (If using olive oil, there is no need to heat it.) Mix in rest of ingredients and sprinkle over halibut. Bake for about 40 minutes.

TOPPING: In saucepan, heat butter or olive oil over medium-low flame and sauté almonds for a few minutes. Sprinkle over fish at serving time.

Sour Cream Dressing

1 cup mayonnaise	2 tsp lemon juice
½ cup sour cream	½ tsp salt
¼ cup chopped dill	¼ tsp black pepper

Mix all the ingredients together and serve with cold fish.

Herbed Mayonnaise Dressing

1 cup mayonnaise	1 Tbsp lemon juice
2 Tbsp mustard	½ cup each chopped parsley and dill

Mix together and serve with cold fish.

Baked Halibut with Sesame Seeds & Almonds

2 lb. (1 kg) piece of halibut, skinned

¼ cup lemon juice

5 cloves garlic, minced

1–2 Tbsp sesame or olive oil

¼ cup lemon juice

2 Tbsp prepared mustard

½ cup thinly sliced scallions

½ tsp salt

½ tsp each thyme and marjoram

½ tsp zatar (optional)

¼ tsp black pepper

1 tsp caraway seeds

2–3 Tbsp sesame seeds

¼ cup lemon juice

¼ cup dry or semidry white wine

¼ cup chopped parsley or dill

OPTIONAL TOPPING

2 Tbsp olive oil

¼ cup almonds, blanched and halved

DRESSING

Red horseradish and mayonnaise

or Mayonnaise Tartar Sauce (see next recipe)

Marinate halibut in ¼ cup lemon juice for an hour, turning once.

Rinse fish and pat dry. Place in baking pan.

Preheat oven to 425°F (220°C).

In jar or food processor mix together garlic, oil, ¼ cup lemon juice, mustard, scallions, salt, thyme, marjoram, zatar and pepper. Pour over fish.

Sprinkle with caraway and sesame seeds.

Pour ¼ cup lemon juice and wine around fish.

Bake uncovered for approximately 40 minutes.

Remove from oven and let stand for 10 minutes.

Remove from pan carefully by inserting two metal spatulas underneath. Transfer fish to serving dish. Sprinkle with parsley or dill.

OPTIONAL TOPPING: Sauté almonds in heated oil over medium-low flame until golden. Sprinkle over fish.

Serve with a mixture of equal amounts of red horseradish and mayonnaise or Mayonnaise Tartar Sauce.

TIME RATIO: Measure width at widest point. 1″ = 8 minutes.

VARIATION: Salmon steaks can be substituted. Bake for 15–20 minutes.

Mayonnaise-Tartar Sauce

½ cup mayonnaise

1 tsp prepared mustard

1 Tbsp scallion, cut up

2 Tbsp chopped parsley

1 pickle, diced

1 Tbsp lemon juice

½ tsp salt

⅛ tsp black pepper

Combine all of the ingredients in bowl and mix together.

Poached or Baked Salmon with Almonds

2 lb. (1 kg) salmon fillet

5 cloves garlic, minced

¼ cup chopped dill

½ tsp salt

⅛ tsp black pepper

1 Tbsp prepared mustard

1 Tbsp lemon juice

1 Tbsp olive oil

2 Tbsp + ½ cup dry or semidry white wine

Preheat oven to 425°F (220°C).

Place salmon in pan.

Make paste out of garlic, dill, salt, pepper, mustard, lemon juice, olive oil and 2 Tbsp wine. Smear paste on salmon. Pour ½ cup wine around salmon.

TO POACH: Cover fish completely with tin foil. Poach for about 20 minutes. Remove from oven and leave covered for about 15 minutes.

TO BAKE: Bake uncovered for about 20 minutes.

If fish weighs more than 2 lb., increase oven time.

TO SERVE: Serve warm with sautéed almonds in butter or Vinaigrette Dressing for Fish (see next recipe), or serve at room temperature with tartar sauce or Mayonnaise-Mustard Dressing (page 63).

P.S. Salmon fillet may be poached all by itself without any trimmings. Simply wrap salmon fillet completely in tin foil and bake as directed above.

TIME RATIO: Measure width at widest point. 1" = 5 minutes. (For whole salmon: 1" = 10 minutes).

Vinaigrette Dressing for Fish

¾ cup olive oil	½ tsp salt
4 cloves garlic, minced	⅛ tsp black pepper
2 Tbsp lemon juice	½ tsp dried tarragon
3 Tbsp vinegar	2 tsp sugar
2 Tbsp chopped parsley	Pinch of cayenne pepper
1 Tbsp capers	(optional)

Process all the ingredients in food processor, or shake in jar. Serve with fish.

Dressing tastes best when fish is sprinkled with blanched, halved almonds.

Honeyed Salmon Steaks

4 salmon steaks

1 tsp butter

1 tsp honey

1 Tbsp brown sugar

2 tsp olive oil

2 tsp lemon juice

2 Tbsp prepared mustard

Wash and pat dry salmon steaks.

In small saucepan melt butter, and stir in honey and sugar.

Add oil, lemon juice and mustard and mix.

Remove from heat and brush sauce on salmon steaks.

Place steaks in flat baking pan side by side. Cover.

Marinate in refrigerator for a few hours.

Microwave for about 7 minutes, or broil for a few minutes on each side.

Sweet & Sour Salmon

6–8 slices of salmon

1 cup tomato juice

2 cups water

1 onion, sliced thin

2 carrots, sliced

¼ tsp salt

⅓ cup vinegar

2 Tbsp lemon juice

⅓ cup sugar

1 Tbsp pickling spices

Rinse salmon slices and set aside.

Place rest of ingredients in pot and cook for 20 minutes.

Add salmon and cook for another ½ hour.

Let cool and refrigerate.

Trout with Almonds

6 trout	1 Tbsp oil
3 Tbsp lemon juice	2 Tbsp vermouth, or dry or semidry white wine
8 cloves garlic, minced	
1 tsp salt	¼ cup (50 g) butter or olive oil
¼ tsp black pepper	¼ cup almonds, blanched and halved

In flat pan leave trout in lemon juice for an hour, turning once.

Rinse under cold water, pat dry and place on broiler pan.

Using a sharp knife, score skin in four places.

Make paste from garlic, salt, pepper, oil and vermouth. Spread ½ on top of trout.

Broil or barbecue for about 15 minutes.

Turn over, score in four places and brush with remaining paste. Broil for 5–10 minutes.

In small saucepan, heat butter or oil and sauté almonds for a few minutes until golden.

Serve with fish.

Poultry & Meat

Roast Chicken with Dried Fruit

A few prunes and apricots

2 Tbsp oil

2 onions, sliced

7 cloves garlic, crushed

2 tsp paprika

1 roasting chicken

5 cloves garlic, crushed

1 Tbsp wine vinegar

2 Tbsp prepared mustard

1 Tbsp paprika

A few small onions or one large onion, quartered

A few small potatoes, whole or cut in half.

Place dried fruit in bowl, pour boiled water over and leave for about ½ hour. Drain.

Sauté onion and garlic in heated oil for about 10 minutes. Add 2 tsp paprika a few minutes into the sautéing.

Clean chicken and pat dry.

In small bowl, mix together garlic, wine vinegar, mustard and paprika. Smear over chicken.

Rinse terra-cotta pan under cold water.

Spread onion mixture on bottom, and place chicken on top of onions.

Spread dried fruit, small onions and potatoes around chicken. Cover baking pan.

Place pan in unheated oven. Turn oven to 350°F (180°C) and bake for 15 minutes.

Increase heat to 425°F (220°C) and continue baking for 1¼ hours.

Remove from oven and place on towel, or wooden or straw trivet (*not* metal). Leave for 10 minutes to settle.

Chicken & Potato Bake

2 Tbsp oil

2 onions, sliced

7 cloves garlic, crushed

2 tsp paprika

½ cup tomato paste (optional)

SEASONING

1 tsp salt

¼ tsp black pepper

2 tsp paprika

½ tsp ginger

2 tsp cumin powder (optional)

3–4 tomatoes, sliced

4 medium potatoes, cut up

1 chicken

Sauté onion and garlic in heated oil about 10 minutes. Add 2 tsp paprika a few minutes into the sautéing.

In small bowl, combine tomato paste and water.

In small bowl, combine seasoning ingredients.

Rinse terra-cotta pan in cold water.

Place ingredients in terra-cotta pan as follows:

- Onions
- Tomatoes
- Tomato paste and water
- Seasoning mixture
- Chicken
- Potatoes (arrange around chicken)

Cover baking pan and place in unheated oven. Turn oven to 350°F (180°C) and bake for 15 minutes.

Increase heat to 425°F (220°C) and continue baking for 1¼ hours.

Remove from oven and place on towel, or wooden or straw trivet (*not* metal). Leave for 10 minutes to settle.

VARIATION: Sprinkle ⅔ cup rice and ⅓ cup lentils over onions and tomatoes.

FOR SLOW COOKING: Leave overnight in oven at 225°F (110°C).

Breaded Baked Chicken with Sesame Seeds

2 small chickens, cut into eighths

MARINADE	COATING
½ cup dry or semidry white wine	¼ cup mayonnaise
¼ cup soy sauce	2 Tbsp prepared mustard
1 tsp paprika	1¼ cups coarsely crushed cornflakes
½ tsp dried rosemary	2 Tbsp sesame seeds
½ tsp ginger	2 tsp garlic powder

Remove skin from chicken pieces. Clean chicken and pat dry.

Mix together marinade ingredients. Pour into large enough pan that the chicken pieces will be able to lay close together in a single layer.

Turn chicken pieces around marinade. Leave in marinade, flesh-side down, overnight in refrigerator.

Remove chicken pieces from marinade, discarding remaining marinade.

Wash and dry baking pan, to prepare it for breaded chicken pieces.

Preheat oven to 350°F (180°C).

In small bowl, combine mayonnaise and mustard.

In separate bowl combine crushed cornflakes, sesame seeds and garlic powder.

Smear each chicken piece with mayonnaise-mustard mixture.

Coat with cornflakes mixture and place in pan.

Bake for about 1¼ hours.

Sweet & Sour Chicken Breasts with Almonds

2 Tbsp oil

2 whole chicken breasts, skinned and boned

1 each green and red pepper, cut into strips

5 cloves garlic, minced

1 Tbsp cornstarch

2 Tbsp soy sauce

1 can (8 oz.; 250 g) pineapple chunks (reserve syrup)

3 Tbsp vinegar

3 Tbsp brown sugar

½ tsp ginger

¼ cup almonds, blanched and halved

Cut chicken breasts into small strips and brown in heated oil in wok or pan.

Add peppers and garlic and continue browning.

Combine cornstarch and soy sauce. Add to pan and stir.

Add pineapple with a little syrup, vinegar, brown sugar, ginger and almonds and sauté for a few minutes.

Serve on linguine, rice or couscous.

Mustard-Coated Chicken Chunks with Walnuts

2 whole chicken breasts, skinned and boned

2 Tbsp prepared mustard

2 Tbsp honey

¼ tsp cayenne pepper (optional)

½ tsp granulated garlic

¾ cup cornstarch

1 Tbsp sesame seeds

2 Tbsp ground walnuts

Preheat oven to 400°F (200°C).

Cut chicken breasts into small chunks.

In small bowl, mix together mustard, honey, cayenne pepper and garlic. Divide into two bowls.

In separate bowl, mix cornstarch, sesame seeds and walnuts.

Dip chicken chunks into one mustard mixture and coat with cornstarch mixture.

Place chicken chunks on greased cookie sheet.

Bake for about 10 minutes, until chicken is tender.

TO SERVE: Place second bowl of mustard mixture on table to be used as a dip.

Chicken-Potato Pie

Marinate schnitzel a few hours before or overnight.

About 1½ lb. (700 g) flat chicken breasts (schnitzel)

MARINADE

4–5 cloves garlic, crushed

2–3 Tbsp olive oil

¼ cup lemon juice

2 tsp honey

¼ tsp salt

⅛ tsp black pepper

½ tsp ginger

1 tsp dried basil (or 2 tsp fresh)

2 Tbsp chopped parsley

1 Tbsp prepared mustard

MASHED POTATOES

1 Tbsp oil

4 cloves garlic, crushed

2 onions, diced

2–3 tsp paprika

3–4 potatoes, cooked

1½ tsp salt

¼ tsp black pepper

CHOPPED CHICKEN

2 Tbsp oil

4 cloves garlic, crushed

2 onions, diced

2 tsp paprika

½ kg (1 lb) chopped chicken

1 Tbsp chopped parsley

1–2 Tbsp ketchup

¼ cup dry red wine

Preheat oven to 350°F (180°C) for 10 minutes before baking.

Place schnitzel in 9" × 13" (23 × 33 cm) flat pan.

Mix marinade ingredients together and smear over schnitzel pieces. Marinate schnitzel a few hours or overnight.

MASHED POTATOES: Sauté garlic and onions in a little oil for about 10 minutes, adding paprika a few minutes into the sautéing. Mash potatoes in bowl. Add onions, salt and pepper.

CHOPPED CHICKEN: Sauté garlic and onions in a little oil for about 10 minutes, adding paprika a few minutes into the sautéing. Add chicken. Using wooden spoon, cut and brown for about 10 minutes. Add parsley, ketchup and wine. Cook, covered, for 10 minutes.

TO ASSEMBLE PIE: Put schnitzel in bowl. Pour remaining marinade over schnitzel. Place potatoes in bottom of pan. Spread chicken over potatoes. Cover chicken with schnitzel pieces.

Bake in oven for 15 minutes.

Shepherd's Pie with Pine Nuts

POTATOES

About 2 lb. (800 g) potatoes, peeled and cooked

1 tsp salt

¼ tsp black pepper

1 Tbsp melted margarine or oil

CHOPPED MEAT

2 Tbsp oil

2 onions, diced

6 cloves garlic, minced

2 tsp paprika

1½ lb. (600 g) chopped meat

2 Tbsp ketchup

1 Tbsp mustard

¼ cup cooked green lentils

2 Tbsp dry red wine

2 Tbsp pine nuts

½ tsp salt

¼ tsp black pepper

2 tsp cumin powder (optional)

Combine potato ingredients, mash and set aside.

Sauté onions and garlic in heated oil for about 10 minutes. Add paprika a few minutes into the sautéing. Stir occasionally.

Preheat oven to 350°F (180°C).

Add rest of ingredients and cook, covered, for about 10 minutes.

Place meat mixture into a 8½" × 11" (21 × 28 cm) shallow baking pan.

Spread mashed potatoes on top.

Sprinkle with additional paprika and bake for about ½ hour.

Sweet Rice Stuffing with Dates & Nuts

½ cup rice

SEASONING

1 tsp salt

¼ tsp black pepper

½ tsp each ginger and dried coriander

¼ tsp cinnamon

1 tsp sugar

2 Tbsp + 1 Tbsp oil

½ cup almonds, blanched and slivered

¼ cup pine nuts

2 Tbsp white raisins

3 cloves garlic, crushed

2 scallions, chopped

2 cups dried dates, cut up

Cook rice and place in bowl.

In small bowl, mix seasoning ingredients. Set aside.

In saucepan, sauté almonds in 2 Tbsp heated oil for a few minutes, stirring continuously.

Add pine nuts and raisins and continue sautéing a couple of minutes, stirring continuously.

Remove with slotted spoon and add to rice.

In same saucepan, sauté garlic in 1 Tbsp heated oil for a few minutes, stirring continuously. Add to rice together with scallions, dates and seasoning and mix.

Plum Sauce with Almonds for Cold Turkey

Prepare a few hours in advance.

1 cup plum preserves

1 small onion, chopped

1 Tbsp vinegar

¼ tsp each of ginger and cinnamon

1 tsp prepared mustard

1 Tbsp almonds, blanched and slivered

In small saucepan, over medium-low flame, bring all of the ingredients to a boil.

Turn off flame and allow to cool.

Serve chilled or at room temperature.

TO SERVE: Sauce may be placed in scooped-out lemon halves and served with cold turkey breast slices. Garnish with melon or orange slices.

Marinades for Poultry

1 whole chicken (quartered) or 2 full chicken breasts (skinned and boned)

MARINADE 1

4 cloves garlic, crushed	⅛ tsp black pepper
3 Tbsp olive oil	1 tsp ginger
¼ cup lemon juice	1 tsp dried basil (or 2 tsp fresh)
2 tsp honey	2 Tbsp chopped parsley
¼ tsp salt	1 Tbsp prepared mustard

MARINADE 2

½ tsp pepper	1 Tbsp honey
1½ tsp ginger	2 Tbsp oil
2 Tbsp soy sauce	½ tsp dried oregano

MARINADE 3

⅓ cup soy sauce	4 cloves garlic, crushed
⅔ cup honey	1 tsp ginger
⅓ cup ketchup	½ tsp dried rosemary
2 Tbsp prepared mustard	

Select marinade and mix all of the ingredients together. (May be done in food processor.)

Smear over chickens and refrigerate a few hours or overnight.

TO GRILL: Turn oven to highest. For quartered chicken, don't grill too close to flame. Grill skin-side down for about 20 minutes, then turn over and grill for another 10 minutes (time depends on size of chicken). Chicken breasts can be grilled closer to heat, a few minutes on each side. Pierce to check for doneness, and remove as soon as there are no raw remnants inside.

Sweet & Sour Turkey Meatballs

CHOPPED TURKEY

2 lb. (1 kg) chopped dark turkey meat (or 1 lb. turkey and 1 lb. chicken)

4 cloves garlic, crushed

1 onion, chopped

3 Tbsp chopped parsley (optional)

2 eggs, slightly beaten

½–¾ cup bread crumbs

2 Tbsp each prepared mustard and ketchup

SAUCE

3 Tbsp olive oil

4 cloves garlic, crushed

2 onions, diced

2 tsp paprika

4 cups homemade Tomato Sauce (see next recipe)

1 tsp salt

¼ tsp black pepper

¼ cup white raisins

⅓ cup lemon juice

¼ cup brown sugar

CHOPPED TURKEY: In bowl, mix everything together and refrigerate for about an hour.

SAUCE: In a 6-quart (6-liter) flat-bottomed pot, heat oil and sauté garlic and onions for about 10 minutes, adding paprika a few minutes into the sautéing. Add rest of ingredients and stir. Heat over medium flame. When it starts to bubble form meatballs (keep hands wet to prevent sticking) and place in sauce.

Cook meatballs for about 2 hours.

After 1 hour gently separate top meatballs.

Tomato Sauce

3 Tbsp olive oil	A few bay leaves
4 cloves garlic, crushed	2 tsp basil
1 large onion, diced	1 tsp salt
2 tsp paprika	¼ tsp black pepper
2 lb. (1 kg) soft tomatoes, cut up	½ tsp ginger
1 small green pepper, cut up	2 tsp sugar
A little chopped parsley	

In pot, heat oil and sauté onion and garlic for about 10 minutes. Add paprika a few minutes into the sautéing.

Add rest of ingredients and cover. Cook over low flame for about ¾ hour, stirring occasionally.

Let cool. Remove bay leaves and blend in blender until smooth, or blend with portable blender in pot.

Apricot-Walnut Sauce

1 cup apricot preserves	¼ cup horseradish
⅓ cup prepared mustard	2 Tbsp chopped walnuts

In saucepan heat apricot preserves, mustard and horseradish.

Add walnuts and stir.

Serve with grilled chicken breasts, chicken or turkey.

Turkey Meatballs with Chili Sauce & Pine Nuts

MEATBALLS

2 lb. (1 kg) chopped dark turkey meat (or 1 lb. turkey and 1 lb. chicken)

5 cloves garlic, crushed

1 onion

1 egg

2–3 slices white or wholewheat bread, soaked and squeezed out,

or about ½ cup bread crumbs

3 Tbsp ketchup

2 Tbsp prepared mustard

¼ tsp each of black pepper and caraway seeds

1–2 tsp cumin powder (optional)

CHILI SAUCE

3 Tbsp oil

5 cloves garlic, crushed

2 onions

2 tsp paprika

1 bottle (about 10 oz; 300 ml) sweet chili sauce

Water, equivalent to chili-sauce amount

1 cup grape or plum jam

Pine nuts

MEATBALLS: Mix meatball ingredients in bowl.

SAUCE: In large, flat-bottomed pot, sauté garlic and onions in heated oil for about 10 minutes, adding paprika a few minutes into the sautéing. Add chili sauce. Fill empty bottle with water and pour into pot. Add jam. Heat and stir together.

Form meatballs and place in pot.

Cook for 2 hours. After about an hour, carefully separate top meatballs.

Serve with pasta or rice. Sprinkle with pine nuts, or add ¼ cup pine nuts to meat mixture.

Quick-Roasted Turkey

1 whole turkey

MARINADE

1–2 Tbsp olive oil (amount depends on size of turkey)

6–8 crushed garlic cloves (amount depends on size of turkey)

apricot and peach jam (use enough to make a nice paste to spread on turkey)

2 Tbsp oil

1 cup semisweet white wine

Preheat oven to 450°F (230°C).

In small bowl, combine marinade ingredients. Smear all over turkey.

Grease roasting pan with 2 Tbsp oil, and put rack inside.

Lay turkey on its side on rack and place in oven.

After ½ hour, pour wine over turkey.

Continue roasting and baste every 20 minutes. (If basting liquid dries up, add a little boiled water.)

After 1¼ hours, turn turkey to other side.

Roast until done. Make sure not to let the breast dry out.

When done, remove from oven. Cover with tin foil and leave for ½ hour.

If bottom is pinkish, broil for a few minutes.

TIME RATIO: 12 lb. (5 kg) turkey = 2 hours; 16 lb. (7 kg) turkey = 2½ hours.

Turkey Strips with Legumes & Walnuts

1 lb. (½ kg) dark turkey meat

2 Tbsp olive oil

5 cloves garlic, minced

1 onion, chopped

1 tsp paprika

¼ cup each walnuts, pine nuts and raisins

2 Tbsp prepared mustard

1 cup rice, cooked

¼ cup each cooked beans (your choice), and cooked lentils

1 tsp salt

¼ tsp black pepper

½ tsp each ginger and turmeric

¼ cup dry red wine

Cut meat into thin strips.

Sauté garlic and onion in heated oil for 10 minutes. Add paprika a few minutes into sautéing.

Add meat and brown for 15–20 minutes, stirring occasionally.

Add rest of ingredients and sauté a few more minutes.

TIP: Cook beans at your leisure, divide into portions and freeze for ready use.

Minced Turkey with Pine Nuts

MEAT MIXTURE

2 lb. (1 kg) minced dark turkey meat (or 1 lb. turkey and 1 lb. chicken)

3 Tbsp ketchup

2 Tbsp prepared mustard

1 tsp cumin powder

¼ cup chopped parsley

½ tsp ginger

¼ tsp black pepper

4 cloves garlic, minced

3 Tbsp oil

4 cloves garlic, minced

2 onions, diced

1 tsp paprika

½ cup cooked beans (your choice)

¾ cup dry red wine

¼ cup each of chopped almonds and pine nuts

½ tsp salt

In bowl, combine ingredients for meat mixture.

In wok or large frying pan, sauté garlic and onions in heated oil for 10 minutes, stirring occasionally. Add paprika a few minutes into the sautéing.

Add meat mixture and continue sautéing for about 15 minutes, until meat browns and separates.

Add beans, wine, almonds, pine nuts and salt. Stir until well blended.

Mushroom Sauce

2 Tbsp margarine or oil

½ lb. (250 g) mushrooms, sliced

2 Tbsp flour

¾ cup water or chicken broth

¼ cup red dry wine

1 tsp salt

¼ tsp each black pepper, thyme and marjoram

Sauté mushrooms in heated margarine or oil for about 10 minutes.

Remove from flame and stir in flour.

Over medium-low flame, add water or broth and wine slowly, stirring continuously.

Stir until thickened.

Add rest of ingredients and mix together.

Cranberry Relish

1 can whole cranberries	½ cup broken-up walnuts
1 cup crushed pineapple	

Combine ingredients in bowl. Serve with poultry.

Turkey-Spinach Roll

1 recipe Plain Pastry I (page 131)

FILLING

1 lb. (½ kg) minced dark turkey meat

5 cloves garlic, crushed

1 Tbsp prepared mustard

2 Tbsp ketchup

1 tsp cumin powder

½ tsp each of dried thyme and marjoram (optional)

¼ cup bread crumbs

1 egg

¼ cup pine nuts

½ lb. (250 g) chopped spinach

2 Tbsp oil

2 onions, chopped

½ lb. (250 g) mushrooms, sliced or diced

GLAZE

1 egg

1 Tbsp water

Sesame seeds

DRESSING

½ cup mayonnaise

½ cup prepared mustard

1 Tbsp Worcestershire Sauce

1 Tbsp lemon juice

Preheat oven to 400°F (200°C).

FILLING: In bowl, mix together minced meat, garlic, mustard, ketchup, cumin, thyme, marjoram, bread crumbs, egg, pine nuts and spinach. Be sure to squeeze out water from the spinach before adding it.

In heated oil, sauté onions for about 7 minutes. Add mushrooms and continue sautéing for 5 minutes. Add meat-spinach mixture and sauté a few minutes more. Allow to cool.

Cut Plain Pastry dough into 3 pieces. Roll out each piece into a rectangular shape.

Spread ⅓ of the meat mixture on each piece. Fold in sides and roll up like jelly roll.

Place on greased cookie sheet.

GLAZE: Mix egg and water and brush over rolls. Sprinkle with sesame seeds. Bake for about 50 minutes.

DRESSING: Mix dressing ingredients together.

TO SERVE: Serve hot with cold dressing.

Turkey-Broccoli-Potato Pie

TOPPING

2 Tbsp oil

5 cloves garlic, crushed

2 onions, diced

2 tsp paprika

½ lb. (250 g) mushrooms, sliced

½ tsp salt

⅛ tsp black pepper

CHOPPED TURKEY

2 Tbsp oil

5 cloves garlic, crushed

1 onion, chopped

2 tsp paprika

2 lb. (1 kg) chopped dark turkey meat (or 1 lb. turkey and 1 lb. chicken)

¼ cup chopped parsley

¼ cup bread crumbs

2 Tbsp each of prepared mustard and ketchup

1 tsp cumin powder

BROCCOLI

1 lb (½ kg) broccoli, cooked and chopped

1 egg

¼ cup bread crumbs

1 small onion, chopped

2 cloves garlic, crushed

1 tsp salt

¼ tsp each black pepper

½ tsp dried coriander

2 Tbsp pine nuts

POTATOES

2 lb. (1 kg) potatoes, cooked and mashed

2 Tbsp margarine

1 tsp salt

¼ tsp black pepper

2 Tbsp chopped dill

Preheat oven to 350°F (180°C).

TOPPING: Sauté garlic and onions in heated oil for about 8 minutes. Add paprika a few minutes into the sautéing. Add mushrooms and sauté for an additional 8–10 minutes. Mix in salt and pepper. Set aside.

CHOPPED TURKEY: Sauté garlic and onions in heated oil for about 10 minutes. Add paprika a few minutes into the sautéing. Mix minced turkey with rest of ingredients, add to onions and brown. Cover and cook for about 5 minutes more.

BROCCOLI: Mix ingredients together.

POTATOES: Mix ingredients together.

Layer in a 9" × 12" (23 × 30 cm) flat baking pan in the following order: turkey, broccoli, potatoes, topping.

Bake for 30–40 minutes.

Allow at least 10 minutes to settle.

Glazed Corned Beef

1 corned beef (about 4 lb.; 2 kg)

GLAZE

2 Tbsp margarine	¼ cup vinegar
⅓ cup ketchup	1 cup brown sugar

Preheat oven to 350°F (180°C).

In large pot, cover corned beef completely with water. Cook, covered, for 2–3 hours until soft. Remove corned beef from pot and place in flat baking pan.

In small saucepan melt margarine. Add ketchup, vinegar and brown sugar and blend well.

Pour over corned beef.

Bake for about 45 minutes, basting every 15 minutes.

Desserts

Pears & Walnuts

7–8 small green pears, cored

SAUCE

½ cup maple syrup

1 Tbsp flaked coconut

¼ cup orange juice

2 Tbsp Cointreau liqueur

¼ cup coarsely chopped walnuts

1 Tbsp lemon juice

1 tsp mint (optional)

Stand pears in a 9" (23 cm) pie plate.

SAUCE: Mix ingredients together and pour over pears.

Cover with plastic wrap. Pierce plastic with a few holes. Microwave for about 10 minutes.

Allow to settle for 10 minutes.

Remove plastic wrap and baste with sauce.

Alternatively, pears can be baked in oven. Preheat oven to 350°F (180°C). Bake for 1 hour.

Pears in Syrup

12 pears, cored

SAUCE

½ cup corn syrup

2 Tbsp fruit liqueur

1 Tbsp lemon juice

1 tsp vanilla extract

½ tsp almond extract

2 Tbsp grated orange rind

¼ cup almonds, blanched and slivered

Stand pears close together in baking dish.

SAUCE: In bowl, microwave corn syrup for ½ minute.

Add liqueur, lemon juice, extracts and orange rind and pour over pears.

Sprinkle with almonds.

Cover with plastic wrap. Pierce plastic with a few holes. Microwave for 15 minutes.

Baste with sauce. Cover again and let stand for 10 minutes.

TO SERVE: Place pears on individual plates and pour sauce over pears.

Baked Apples & Nuts

5 Granny Smith apples

NUT MIXTURE

¼ cup brown sugar

¼ tsp cinnamon

½ cup ground almonds

¼ cup ground walnuts

2 Tbsp butter, melted

¾ cup hot water

¼ cup honey

1 tsp vanilla extract

2 Tbsp lemon juice

Preheat oven to 425°F (220°C).

Peel and core apples.

In small bowl, mix nut mixture together.

Grease deep-dish pie pan.

Smear apples with melted butter.

Roll in nut mixture and place in pan.

Spoon remaining nut mixture into apple cores and then over apples.

Combine hot water, honey, vanilla extract and lemon juice and pour on bottom of pan.

Bake, covered, for 30 minutes. Uncover, baste and bake for 10 minutes more.

Baste again.

TO SERVE: Place apples on rimmed plate, pour a little juice on apples and encircle with a little sweet cream or whipped cream.

Brandied Apples & Walnuts

6 Granny Smith apples, peeled and cored

3 Tbsp lemon juice

¼ cup margarine, melted

¼ cup sugar

3 Tbsp brandy

2 Tbsp chopped walnuts

Preheat oven to 350°F (180°C).

Cut apples into wedges and toss in lemon juice.

In separate large bowl, mix rest of ingredients.

Using slotted spoon, add apples and mix.

Place in large, flat baking dish.

Bake 1 hour, turning once after ½ hour.

SUGGESTION: Serve with Orange Pound Cake and ice cream.

Peach Delight

2 lb. (1 kg) peaches (approximately 5–6 peaches), skinned, pitted and cut up

½ cup orange juice

1 tsp grated orange rind

½ cup sweet red wine

¼ cup sugar

3 Tbsp cornstarch

¼ cup each flaked coconut and broken-up pecan nuts

TO SKIN PEACHES: Place in boiled water, turn off flame and for leave 15–20 seconds.

Throw into colander and rinse under cold water. Skin should peel off easily.

Process peaches, orange juice, orange rind, wine, sugar and cornstarch in food processor. Transfer to pot and cook over low heat for 8–10 minutes, stirring occasionally.

Chill and serve.

Sprinkle each portion with coconut and pecans.

Winter Fruit Salad

Preferable to prepare a day or two in advance.

2 navel oranges, sectioned without membrane

½–1 small melon

2 pears

2 square persimmons (they're softer)

2 kiwi

4 dates

¼ cup flaked coconut

⅔ cup Curaçao Triple Sec *clear* liqueur

2 Tbsp brandy

Coarsely chopped walnuts or pecan nuts

Ice cream or whipped cream

TO SECTION ORANGES: Peel and cut in between membranes.

Use only ripe fruit. Peel and cut up melon, pears, persimmons and kiwi into bowl.

Add cut-up dates, coconut, Triple Sec and brandy and mix well.

Sprinkle nuts over individual portions.

Top with ice cream or whipped cream.

NOTE: ½ cup Cointreau liqueur can be substituted for Curacao Triple Sec. Other fruits in season can be substituted or added (e.g., strawberries, bananas, red apples).

Summer Fruit Salad

Preferable to prepare a day or two in advance.

½–1 small melon	¼ cup flaked coconut
3 peaches	⅔ cup Curaçao Triple Sec, *clear liqueur*
4 plums	
2 mangoes	2 Tbsp brandy
A bunch of grapes (optional)	Coarsely chopped walnuts
4 dates	Ice cream or whipped cream

Use only ripe fruit. Cut up melon, peaches, plums, grapes and dates into bowl.

Add coconut, Curaçao and brandy and mix well.

Sprinkle walnuts over individual portions.

Top with ice cream or whipped cream

NOTE: ½ cup Cointreau liqueur can be substituted for Curaçao. Other fruits in season can be added.

Baked Goodies

Plain Pastry I

Good for food pies and rolls, quiches and lemon meringue pie.

2⅓ cups flour

½ tsp baking powder

¼ tsp salt

¾ cup cold butter or margarine

About ½ cup ice water

Sift together flour, baking powder and salt. Cut in butter.

Add ice water and knead until soft dough is formed. Don't overknead.

Alternatively, this may be done in food processor with metal blade: Process flour and butter a few seconds. Add ice water slowly and process a few more seconds. Stop processor as soon as glob of dough is formed. Knead a few seconds on floured board to form ball of dough. Don't overknead.

Plain Pastry II

2⅓ cups flour

½ tsp baking powder

¼ tsp salt

½ cup (100 g) cold margarine

1 egg

½ cup cold water

Process the same as Plain Pastry I.

When intended for food rolls, smear dough with slightly beaten egg white after rolling out.

NOTE: Dough can be frozen for ready use.

Cookie Dough

Good for fruit pie crust and filled rolled cake.

About 4 cups flour

1 Tbsp baking powder

¼ tsp salt

¾ cup sugar

¾ cup oil

3 eggs

⅓ cup orange juice

In bowl sift flour, baking powder and salt. Set aside.

In mixing bowl beat sugar and oil. Add eggs and orange juice. Beat a few seconds.

Lower speed and add flour slowly. Beat until dough is formed.

Freeze 1 hour, or refrigerate overnight.

Filled Rolled Cake

Cookie Dough (see previous recipe)

FILLING

1 cup ground walnuts

¼ cup sugar

1 Tbsp cinnamon

2 Tbsp flaked coconut

½ cup raisins

4 Tbsp apricot or plum jam

Preheat oven to 350°F (180°C).

In bowl, mix together filling ingredients.

Cut cookie dough into 4 pieces. Roll out each piece. Spread each piece with 1 Tbsp jam. Sprinkle each piece with ¼ of the filling. Roll up.

Place on greased cookie sheets.

Bake for about 35 minutes.

Pecan Pie

⅓ recipe Plain Pastry I (page 131)

½ cup butter, room temperature

½ cup sugar

¾ cup corn syrup

¼ cup maple syrup or honey

3 eggs

1 tsp vanilla extract

2 cups pecan nuts (1 cup broken up; 1 cup pecan halves)

Preheat oven to 425°F (220°C).

Roll out dough on floured board and place in a 9" (23 cm) round pie plate. Flute edges.

In mixer, at medium speed, beat butter and sugar until creamy.

Lower speed and slowly add syrup, eggs (one at a time), vanilla and broken pecans.

Pour mixture into pie shell.

Arrange pecan halves neatly on top.

Bake for 10 minutes.

Lower heat to 350°F (180°C) and continue baking for another 30–35 minutes.

Serve with ice cream and/or whipped cream.

Homemade Corn Syrup

2 Tbsp water	½ cup sugar

Cook water and sugar in small saucepan over low-medium flame until caramelized. Do not stir. Syrup must be used as soon as it is made. It may harden when adding it to the mixer, but in the baking it will melt again.

Makes ½ cup corn syrup.

Blueberry Pie

Cookie Dough (amount used depends on desired thickness of crust)	½ cup sugar
	1 Tbsp cornstarch
	2 Tbsp apricot preserves
2 Tbsp chopped walnuts	½ tsp cinnamon
FILLING	2 Tbsp lemon juice
6 cups blueberries	1 Tbsp lemon rind

Preheat oven to 350°F (180°C).

Roll out enough dough for a 10" (25 cm) deep-dish pie pan.

Spread chopped walnuts over pie crust.

In large bowl, mix together filling ingredients and pour into pie pan.

Roll out enough cookie dough to cover filling. Perforate crust with fork.

Bake for about an hour until crust is golden brown.

P.S. Any leftover cookie dough can be frozen or used for Filled Rolled Cake.

Banana-Walnut Cake

2 cups flour	2 eggs
½ tsp baking powder	1 tsp vanilla extract
¾ tsp baking soda	¼ tsp almond extract
Pinch of salt	¼ cup orange juice
2 Tbsp flaked coconut (optional)	2 Tbsp walnuts, coarsely chopped
½ cup butter, room temperature	
1½ cups sugar	1 cup (3–4) bananas, mashed

Preheat oven to 350°F (180°C).

In bowl sift flour, baking powder, baking soda and salt. Add coconut and set aside.

In mixer, at medium speed, beat butter and sugar for 1 minute.

Add eggs and extracts and continue beating for a few minutes until thickened.

Lower speed to lowest and add flour mixture alternately with juice. Beat just until last of flour is added. Fold in walnuts and bananas.

Pour batter into greased loaf pan.

Bake for about 50 minutes.

Butterscotch Brownies

1 cup flour

1 Tbsp baking powder

¼ tsp salt

2 Tbsp flaked coconut (optional)

½ cup (100 g) butter, room temperature

2 cups brown sugar

2 eggs

2 tsp vanilla extract

1 cup walnuts, coarsely chopped

Preheat oven to 350°F (180°C).

In bowl sift flour, baking powder and salt. Add coconut and set aside.

In small saucepan, melt butter and stir in brown sugar.

Place in mixing bowl and beat at medium speed, adding eggs and vanilla extract.

Lower speed to lowest and add flour mixture. Turn off mixer and fold in walnuts.

Spread into greased 8" (20 cm) square baking pan and bake for about 30 minutes.

Brownies with Fudge Frosting

⅔ cup flour

1 tsp baking powder

¼ tsp salt

½ cup cocoa

2 Tbsp flaked coconut

½ cup butter, room temperature

1 cup sugar

2 eggs

1 tsp vanilla extract

½ cup walnuts, coarsely chopped

Preheat oven to 350°F (180°C).

In bowl, sift flour, baking powder, salt and cocoa. Add coconut and set aside.

In mixer, at medium speed, beat butter and sugar.

Add eggs, one at a time, and vanilla extract, and beat a few minutes until smooth.

Lower speed to lowest and add flour mixture.

Turn off mixer as soon as last of flour is added. Fold in walnuts.

Place in 8" (20 cm) square baking pan.

Bake for about 30 minutes.

Cool and frost with Fudge Frosting (see next recipe).

Fudge Frosting

3 Tbsp butter, room temperature

1 egg yolk

2 tsp coffee liquid or milk

1 tsp vanilla extract

1 cup powdered sugar, sifted

3 Tbsp cocoa

Beat in mixer until smooth. Spread over brownies.

Chocolate Chip Squares

2½ cups flour

1 cup flaked coconut

½ cup walnuts, coarsely chopped

1 cup sugar

½ cup brown sugar

1 cup oil

2 eggs

1 tsp vanilla extract

1 cup chocolate chips

Preheat oven to 350°F (180°C).

Sift flour into bowl. Add coconut and walnuts and set aside.

In mixer, at medium speed, beat sugars and oil.

Add eggs, one at a time, and vanilla extract, and beat for a few minutes until smooth.

Lower speed to lowest and add flour mixture.

Turn off mixer as soon as last of flour is added. Fold in chocolate chips.

Spread into a greased 9" (23 cm) square baking pan. Bake for 20–25 minutes.

Fudge Cake with Pears & Walnuts

2 cups flour

2 tsp baking soda

¼ tsp salt

¾ cup cocoa

¼ cup flaked coconut

1½ cups sugar

¾ cup butter, room temperature

3 eggs

2 tsp vanilla extract

¼ tsp almond extract

1½ cups buttermilk, or 1 cup strong coffee + 2 Tbsp coffee liqueur

¼ cup walnuts, chopped

3 pears, peeled, cored and grated

Preheat oven to 350°F (180°C).

In bowl, sift flour, baking soda, salt and cocoa. Add coconut and set aside.

In mixer, at medium speed, beat sugar and butter.

Add eggs, one at a time, and extracts, and beat a few minutes until thick.

Lower speed to lowest and add flour mixture alternately with liquid. (1½ cups buttermilk = 3 Tbsp vinegar and 1 cup + 5 Tbsp milk.)

Turn off mixer as soon as last of flour is added. Fold in walnuts and pears.

Pour into greased 10" (25 cm) tube pan.

Bake for about an hour. Frost with desired glaze or frosting.

Orange Pound Cake

2 cups flour

3 tsp baking powder

Pinch of salt

2 Tbsp flaked coconut

1¼ cup sugar

⅔ cup oil

3 eggs

1½ tsp vanilla extract

¼ tsp almond extract

⅔ cup orange juice

1 Tbsp lemon juice

Preheat oven to 350°F (180°C).

In bowl, sift flour, baking powder and salt. Add coconut and set aside.

In mixer, at medium speed, beat sugar and oil.

Add eggs, one at a time, and extracts, and beat a few minutes until thick.

Lower speed to lowest and add flour mixture alternately with juices.

Turn off mixer as soon as last of flour is added.

With wooden spoon continue mixing until just blended.

Pour batter into greased loaf pan. Bake for 1–1¼ hours.

3-Tier Chocolate Cake

1 cup cocoa

2 cups water

2¾ cups flour

½ tsp baking powder

2 tsp baking soda

½ tsp salt

2 Tbsp flaked coconut

1 cup (200–240 g) margarine, room temperature

1½ cups sugar

4 eggs

2 tsp vanilla extract

Cocoa Icing (see next recipe)

Preheat oven to 350°F (180°C).

Combine cocoa and water and refrigerate overnight.

In bowl, sift flour, baking powder, baking soda and salt. Add coconut and set aside.

In mixer, at medium speed, beat margarine and sugar.

Add eggs, one at a time, and vanilla extract, and beat a few minutes until thick.

Lower speed to lowest and add flour mixture alternately with cocoa mixture.

Turn off mixer as soon as last of flour is added. Finish mixing with wooden spoon.

Pour equal amounts into 3 layer-cake pans (8"; 20 cm) and bake for 25–30 minutes.

Ice each layer with Cocoa Icing. Assemble iced layers on top of each other to create 3-tier cake.

Cocoa Icing

2 cups powdered sugar

¼ cup cocoa

1 Tbsp flaked coconut (optional)

About ¼ cup hot water

¼ cup oil

1 tsp vanilla extract

Combine all of the ingredients in mixer or mix with wooden spoon. (If too thick, add a little more hot water).

Carrot Cake

2 cups flour

2 tsp baking powder

2 tsp baking soda

1 Tbsp cinnamon

½ tsp salt

1 tsp ginger

¾ cup flaked coconut

1¼ cups oil

¾–1 cup white sugar

1 cup brown sugar

3 eggs

1 Tbsp vanilla extract

½ cup applesauce

2 cups (about 4) carrots, grated

½ cup crushed pineapple

½ cup pecan nuts, coarsely chopped

¼ cup raisins

Preheat oven to 350°F (180°C).

In bowl, sift flour, baking powder, baking soda, cinnamon, salt and ginger.

Add coconut and set aside.

In mixer, at medium speed, beat oil and sugars.

Add eggs, one at a time, and vanilla extract, and beat a few minutes until thick.

Lower speed to lowest and add flour mixture alternately with applesauce.

Turn off mixer as soon as last of flour is added.

With wooden spoon, fold in carrots, pineapple, pecan nuts and raisins.

Place in greased tube or Bundt pan and bake for about 1¼ hours.

Frost with Cream-Cheese Frosting or Orange Glaze (see next recipes).

Cream-Cheese Frosting

2 cups cream cheese	2½–3 cups powdered sugar
½ cup butter, room temperature	1 Tbsp lemon juice
1 Tbsp vanilla extract	1 Tbsp lemon rind

In mixer beat cream cheese and butter. Add vanilla.

Add powdered sugar gradually.

Add lemon juice and rind and beat until reaches frosting consistency.

Spread over Carrot Cake.

Orange Glaze

½ cup powdered sugar	1 tsp vanilla extract
About 1 Tbsp orange juice and 1 tsp lemon juice	

Place powdered sugar in bowl. Add juices and extract and mix.

Adjust amount of juices to attain drippy consistency.

Pour slowly over top of cooled cake, allowing it to drip a little over sides.

Chocolate Cream Frosting

½ cup whipping cream

1 cup powdered sugar

½ cup cream cheese

2 tsp vanilla extract

1 Tbsp cocoa powder

1 Tbsp flaked coconut (optional)

In mixer with whipping blade, at medium-high speed, whip whipping cream.

Add rest of ingredients, one at a time, and beat until smooth and thick.

If not thick enough, refrigerate for an hour before frosting cake.

Chocolate Frosting

¼ cup butter or margarine

1 cup (6 oz.; 180 g) bittersweet chocolate

½ cup milk or coffee

1 tsp vanilla extract

About 2¼ cups powdered sugar

Pinch of salt

In small saucepan melt butter and bittersweet chocolate, stirring continuously.

Mix vanilla into milk or coffee.

In mixer, at lowest speed, beat powdered sugar and salt while adding chocolate-butter mixture.

Add milk-vanilla mixture. Increase speed to medium-high and beat until smooth.

Pour frosting over cupcakes.

Chocolate-Maple Frosting

¼ cup (50 g) butter

1 cup (6 oz.; 180 g) bittersweet chocolate

2–3 Tbsp maple syrup

In small saucepan melt butter, chocolate and maple syrup. Pour over cupcakes.

Speedy Frosting

Place one square of chocolate on each cupcake when removing from oven.

Allow each square to melt for about 30 seconds and then spread over cupcake.

Chocolate Icing

1 cup sugar

¼ cup cocoa

¾ cup cornstarch

1 cup hot water

1 Tbsp margarine

2 Tbsp flaked coconut

1 tsp vanilla extract

In bowl mix together sugar, cocoa and cornstarch.

Slowly add hot water, stirring continuously. Stir until thick.

Add margarine, coconut and vanilla extract and stir until well blended.

Chocolaty Cupcakes

1¾ cup flour

1½ tsp baking powder

1½ tsp baking soda

½ tsp salt

2 Tbsp flaked coconut

1 cup cocoa

2 cups sugar

2 eggs

¾ cup sweet cream

¼ cup water

½ cup oil

1 tsp vanilla extract

1 cup boiling water

Preheat oven to 375°F (190°C).

Sift flour, baking powder, baking soda and salt into mixing bowl. Add coconut, cocoa and sugar.

Start beating at medium-low speed. Add rest of ingredients, one at a time.

Beat just until blended. Mix a little with wooden spoon.

Pour into paper-lined cupcake tins, until ⅔ full.

Bake for about 15 minutes.

Frost with desired frosting.

Almond-Chip Cookies

1¼ cups flour

½ tsp baking powder

Pinch of salt

2 Tbsp flaked coconut

½ cup sugar

¾ cup (150–175 g) butter, room temperature

⅓ cup ground almonds

1 tsp vanilla extract

1 egg

½ cup (3½ oz.; 100 g) chocolate chips

Preheat oven to 400°F (200°C).

In bowl, sift flour, baking powder and salt. Add coconut and set aside.

In mixer, at medium speed, beat sugar and butter.

Add rest of ingredients and beat until smooth.

Drop by tablespoonfuls onto greased cookie sheets, allowing room for spreading.

Remove immediately onto flat surface. Cookies will harden within 10 minutes.

Blondies

2½ cups flour

2½ tsp baking powder

2 cups brown sugar

3 eggs

⅔ cup oil

¼ cup orange juice

1 tsp vanilla

1 cup chopped walnuts

2 cups chocolate chips

Preheat oven to 350°F (180°C).

Place all ingredients in mixer, and beat for about 4 minutes.

Place in greased, lipped cookie sheet and bake for about ½ hour.

Cut while still warm.

Sesame Crescents

1½ cups + 2 Tbsp flour

¼ tsp baking soda

Pinch of salt

1 Tbsp flaked coconut

½ cup brown sugar

½ cup butter, room temperature

1 egg + 1 egg yolk

1 tsp vanilla extract

¼ tsp almond extract

1 Tbsp brandy

2 Tbsp ground walnuts

TOPPING

½ cup sesame seeds

3 Tbsp sugar

Preheat oven to 375°F (190°C).

In bowl, sift flour, baking soda and salt. Add coconut and set aside.

In mixer, at medium speed, beat sugar and butter one minute.

Add egg, egg yolk and extracts and beat until thick.

Lower speed to lowest, add flour mixture, brandy and walnuts and beat until smooth.

Knead a little by hand until soft but not sticky dough is formed.

In bowl, mix together topping ingredients.

Take a small glob of dough, and with palm of hand form a ball and then into a thick log. Form crescent shape by bending slightly. Continue until all the dough is used. Dip each crescent into topping and place on greased cookie sheets.

Bake for about 10 minutes.

Oatmeal-Date Chocolate Chip Cookies

½ cup flour

1 tsp each of baking powder and baking soda

⅛ tsp salt

1½ cups oatmeal

2 Tbsp flaked coconut

⅔ cup brown sugar

½ cup sugar

½ cup (100 g) butter, room temperature

1 egg

1 tsp vanilla extract

¾ cup each of pitted chopped dates, chopped pecans and semisweet chocolate chips

Preheat oven to 375°F (190°C).

In bowl, sift flour, baking powder, baking soda and salt. Add oatmeal and coconut and set aside.

In mixer, at medium speed, beat sugars and butter for 1 minute.

Add egg and vanilla extract, and beat until fluffy.

Lower speed to lowest, and add oatmeal mixture.

Using wooden spoon, fold in dates, pecans and chocolate chips.

Drop by tablespoonfuls onto greased cookie sheets. Flatten with fork.

Bake for about 10 minutes.

Allow to cool for 5 minutes before placing on rack to cool completely.

Apple Bran Muffins

½ cup (100 g) butter, melted

¼ cup brown sugar

1 Tbsp honey

2 eggs

¼ cup buttermilk

½ cup bran

¾ cup wholewheat flour

1 cup white flour

2 tsp each of baking powder and baking soda

½ tsp each of cinnamon and salt

2 Tbsp flaked coconut

½ cup each raisins and ground walnuts

2 dates, cut up (optional)

1 cup thick, unsweetened, applesauce

Preheat oven to 400°F (200°C).

In bowl, mix together butter, sugar, honey, eggs, buttermilk and bran. (¼ cup buttermilk = 1 tsp vinegar + enough milk to make ¼ cup. Let stand for a few minutes.)

In separate bowl, sift together flour, baking powder, baking soda, cinnamon and salt.

Add buttermilk-bran mixture to flour together with rest of ingredients.

Mix with wooden spoon just until blended.

Place batter in greased muffin tins almost to the tops. Bake for 12–15 minutes.

Nutty Muffins

¾ cup walnuts, coarsely chopped

2 cups white flour, *or* 1 cup wholewheat flour + ¾ cup white flour

1 Tbsp baking powder

1 tsp baking soda

½ tsp salt

⅔ cup brown sugar

2 Tbsp flaked coconut

2 eggs

1 cup buttermilk

1 tsp vanilla extract

½ cup (100 g) butter, melted

¼ cup raisins

2 ripe bananas, mashed, *or* two pears, peeled and grated

Preheat oven to 400°F (200°C).

Microwave walnuts for 1½ minutes. Set aside.

In bowl sift flour, baking powder, baking soda and salt. Add brown sugar and coconut.

In separate bowl whisk eggs and stir in buttermilk and vanilla. (¼ cup buttermilk = 1 tsp vinegar + enough milk to make ¼ cup. Let stand for a few minutes.)

Add to flour mixture together with butter, raisins and bananas (or pears). Using wooden spoon, mix everything together.

Spoon into greased muffin tins almost to the tops.

Bake for about 15 minutes.

Carrot Muffins

½ cup wholewheat flour

½ cup white flour

1 tsp baking soda

¼ tsp salt

1 tsp cinnamon

2 Tbsp flaked coconut

2 eggs

¾ cup sugar

¼ cup oil

1 tsp vanilla extract

1 cup (about 2) grated carrots

⅓ cup thick applesauce

¼ cup chopped pecans or almonds

¼ cup raisins

Preheat oven to 400°F (200°C).

Sift flour, baking soda, salt and cinnamon. Add coconut and set aside.

In separate, larger bowl whisk eggs. Add sugar, oil and vanilla and whisk a little more.

Add flour mixture, carrots, applesauce, nuts and raisins.

Using wooden spoon, mix just until blended. Don't overbeat.

Grease 12 cupcake tins and fill ¾ full.

Bake for about 15 minutes.

Corn-Walnut Muffins

1 cup flour	⅓ cup butter, melted
4 tsp baking powder	1 cup buttermilk
½ tsp salt	2 eggs, slightly beaten
2 Tbsp flaked coconut (optional)	1 tsp vanilla extract
1 cup cornmeal	¼ cup chopped walnuts
⅓ cup sugar	

Preheat oven to 400°F (200°C).

In large bowl sift flour, baking powder and salt. Add rest of ingredients and mix. (1 cup buttermilk = 2 Tbsp vinegar + enough milk to make 1 cup. Let stand for a few minutes.)

Pour batter into greased cupcake tins, almost to top, and bake for 12–15 minutes.

TOPPING: Melt ¼ cup butter. Stir in ¼ tsp cinnamon and spread over muffins when done.

Scone Wedges

2 cups flour	2 Tbsp each ground walnuts and raisins
2 tsp baking powder	
½ tsp baking soda	⅓ cup butter, cut up
¼ tsp each salt and cinnamon	2 eggs
½ cup sugar	
2 Tbsp flaked coconut	⅔ cup buttermilk
½ cup cornmeal	2 tsp vanilla extract
	¼ tsp almond extract

Preheat oven to 350°F (180°C).

In large bowl sift flour, baking powder, baking soda, salt and cinnamon.

Add sugar, coconut, cornmeal, walnuts and raisins.

Add butter and mix with hands, forming a crumbly mixture.

In separate bowl, whisk eggs together with buttermilk and extracts. (⅔ cup buttermilk = 1 Tbsp vinegar + enough milk to made ⅔ cup. Let stand for a few minutes.)

Don't overmix. Mixture can be a little lumpy.

Spread on greased springform pan. Bake for about 25 minutes.

When cooled, cut into wedges by cutting across circumference horizontally and vertically. Then cut each wedge according to desired size.

Cheese Swirls

2 cups flour	2 Tbsp ground peanuts
2 tsp baking powder	¼ cup butter, room temperature
1 tsp salt	½ cup milk
⅛ tsp pepper	1 cup grated cheese
1 Tbsp caraway seeds	

Preheat oven to 350°F (180°C).

In bowl sift flour, baking powder, salt and pepper. Add caraway seed and peanuts. Cut in butter.

Add milk and form soft, but not sticky, dough. Divide dough in half.

On floured board, roll out each half. Sprinkle with grated cheese and roll up.

Cut into thick slices and place, flat side down, on greased cookie sheet.

Bake for about 20 minutes.

Cheese Sticks

1½ cups flour

Pinch of cayenne pepper (optional)

¼ tsp salt

½ cup (100 g) butter

1 cup Cheddar cheese, grated

2 Tbsp each of sesame seeds and caraway seeds

1 Tbsp chopped walnuts

1 egg yolk

3 Tbsp water

Preheat oven to 375°F (190°C).

Sift together flour, cayenne pepper and salt. Cut in butter.

Add rest of ingredients and knead until soft, but not sticky, dough is formed.

Divide dough in half and roll out each half to medium thickness.

Trim sides so that they are straight.

Cut lengthwise into strips. Cut each strip into desired length.

Place on greased cookie sheet. Bake for 12–15 minutes.

Index

Salads

Soups

Vegetables